Daily Advent Reflections

Nick Fawcett

**kevin
mayhew**

First published in 2003 by
KEVIN MAYHEW LTD
Buxhall, Stowmarket, Suffolk, IP14 3BW
E-mail: info@kevinmayhewltd.com

KINGSGATE PUBLISHING INC
1000 Pannell Street, Suite G, Columbia, MO 65201
E-mail: sales@kingsgatepublishing.com

9 8 7 6 5 4 3 2 1

ISBN 184417 141 8
Catalogue No 1500632

Cover design by Jo Balaam
Edited by Katherine Laidler
Typesetting by Louise Selfe
Printed in Great Britain

Contents

Fourth week of Advent: A time to respond

Christmas week: A time to celebrate

Introduction

The first Sunday of Advent: for many that date in the Christian calendar is a special one, stirring the imagination, kindling memories and heralding a season of challenge and promise that culminates in the joyful celebration of Christmas. No other time quite captures the public imagination as this one does, and many who would not otherwise dream of attending worship do so at some point over the season. Is it just sentiment and tradition? Partly, perhaps, but not entirely. Is it a love of Christmas carols, candlelight services and festive cheer? That, too, is certainly a factor, but by no means the whole story. Is it a desire to bring some light and magic into the dreary days of winter? That may well be so for some, but I don't think so for all. Accuse me of naivety if you like, but I believe many genuinely yearn to discover a spiritual dimension to life, and the Christmas season, albeit briefly, opens up a window through which they can catch a glimpse of the divine.

What, then, is so special about this time of year? That's what this book sets out to explore. Written for all who want to reflect more deeply on the significance of God's coming in Christ, it provides readings, reflections, prayers and points to ponder arranged around five themes, one for each week of Advent and another for the week including Christmas. These, in turn, revolve around three axes: what God has done, what he is doing, and what he has yet to do. We consider the hope of Advent, asking whether our expectations need to be stretched, opened to new horizons. We ask in what way we need to prepare ourselves to welcome Christ into our lives, both now and on his final return in glory. We reflect on why Advent gives us grounds to trust in God despite everything that life may throw at us. We look at the response people made to Christ at the time of his birth and the response we are called to make in turn. Finally, we explore in what ways the coming of Christ is good news for today. The aim is to provide material for a short but meaningful act of devotion throughout the season of Advent and the first week of Christmas – devotions that

5

will at once challenge, encourage, nurture and inspire. My hope is that something in these pages may open the window on this special time, affording a clearer glimpse of God's love in Christ, the one at its heart.

NICK FAWCETT

To Harry and Margaret Manifold,
with grateful memories of times shared

First week of Advent

A time to expect

The week ahead

'May I ask what you were expecting to see out of a Torquay hotel bedroom window. Sydney Opera House, perhaps? The Hanging Gardens of Babylon? Herds of wildebeest sweeping majestically [across the plains of Africa]?' Fans of the classic comedy series *Fawlty Towers* will recognise those words immediately. They come from the instalment titled 'Communication Problems' and are addressed by the inimitable John Cleese (alias Basil Fawlty) to an elderly guest who complains that the view from her room is not quite what she had in mind. The question, of course, is deliberately taken to ludicrous extremes, but its thrust takes us to the heart of Advent for this is a season that asks each of us what we are expecting in relation to life and in relation to Christ. On one level, it calls us to look ahead to Christmas and to prepare ourselves to celebrate again the birth of Christ. It calls us also to remember the expectation felt by the people of Israel as they looked forward to the coming of the Messiah in fulfilment of ancient words of prophecy. Above all, though, it calls us to anticipate the return of Christ in glory to establish God's kingdom and fulfil his age-long purpose. It sounds simple enough, but, as the coming of Jesus in Bethlehem and his subsequent ministry remind us, many were taken by surprise by the sort of Messiah he proved to be. Advent, then, is not simply a time for expecting but a time also for asking ourselves whether we are expecting the right thing; whether we are open to what God has done, is doing, and has yet to do.

Day 1: Open to the unexpected

Approach

Sovereign God,
   I bring you my fractured, feeble faith.
Strengthen and nurture it,
   so that I may know you more fully,
   love you more deeply
   and serve you more truly.
Amen.

Read

No one – not even the angels in heaven or the Son – knows the details of that day and hour; only the Father knows. The coming of the Son of Man will be akin to the time of Noah, in the days leading up to the flood. Just as they carried on then with life as normal – eating, drinking, marrying and so forth – having no inkling of the impending catastrophe until it engulfed them, so it will be with the Son of Man's coming. For example, two people will be working in a field; one will be taken up but the other left standing there. Two women will be pounding grain together; once more, one will be taken and the other left alone. Stay alert, then, for you have no idea what day your Lord may come. You need to remember this: that if the victim of a burglary had known when the thief would strike, he would have stayed awake to prevent it happening. Similarly, you should be prepared, for the hour of the Son of Man's coming will come as a complete surprise.
Matthew 24:36-44

Reflect

The secret of a whodunit novel, so I am told, is to keep the reader guessing right to the very end. We may think we know who committed the crime, only to be taken by surprise when the culprit's identity is finally revealed. It may prove to be the least likely person, or it may be that the suspect whom we've dismissed as being too obvious turns out to be the guilty party after all. Quite simply, we're never sure what to expect.

There's a parallel here with New Testament accounts of the last days and the return of Christ, for here too we are dealing with the unexpected. As Jesus himself told the Apostles, in response to questions concerning his return and the establishment of his kingdom, no one knows when or where this will be. Many have mistakenly assumed they do, predicting the end of the world or the second coming at such and such a date, but their confidence has been exposed as misplaced. We can push the lesson further, for it applies to the things of God in general. As the prophet Isaiah reminds us, 'God's ways are not our ways nor are his thoughts our thoughts' – a truth that has been demonstrated on innumerable occasions. The people of Israel in the days of Amos believed that faithful observance of religious feasts and worship was all it took to keep God happy. They were in for a rude awakening, as God declared his contempt for any so-called devotion divorced from a commitment to justice. Jews at the time of Jesus yearned for a political Messiah who would deliver them from earthly oppression. They could make no sense of a Saviour crucified as a common criminal. Simon Peter was convinced that Gentiles were ritually unclean and therefore outside of God's purpose. Events were to prove him wrong, Gentiles very clearly being touched by God's Spirit. Paul believed Jesus to be a blasphemer against the Jewish Law, yet came eventually to see him as its fulfilment. So it has continued throughout history. Countless generations have been surprised by God acting in news ways, overturning expectations, challenging preconceived ideas, stretching horizons, reshaping faith. He cannot be tied down to narrow human horizons. That's why I've always been suspicious of attempts to encapsulate Christian belief in statements of faith or articles of dogma, whether old or new. We do not know all there is to know of God, nor will we ever do. We cannot understand the breadth of his purpose, the extent of his love or the scope of his mercy, nor, in this life should we for a moment presume we ever will. God repeatedly speaks in ways we never expect, revealing aspects of his nature we've never considered and calling us to avenues of service we've never contemplated. Are we open to that God of surprises, our God of the unexpected?

Pray

I prayed, Lord.
I watched and I waited,
    trusting,
    expecting,
    hoping . . .
    but nothing happened.
I prayed again,
    crying out for help,
    pleading for guidance,
    and this time I was not only sure you'd answer
    but also confident of what the answer would be.
Only it wasn't what I expected,
    life taking an unforeseen twist,
    shattering my illusions,
    crushing my hopes,
    and leaving faith teetering,
    balanced over a precipice.
I called again,
    begging you this time,
    promising you undying loyalty,
    total commitment,
    if you would just respond to my plea . . .
    but yet again the answer was wanting,
    and I felt lost,
    confused,
    frightened;
    everything that had seemed so certain suddenly so insecure.

But then you spoke –
  through the counsel of a friend,
  the testimony of Scripture,
  the prompting of your Spirit,
  the circumstances of life –
  and I realised you'd been speaking all along,
  giving your reply,
  except the answer was different from the one I'd looked for,
  your purpose breaking out of the fetters I'd placed upon it,
  refusing to be confined.
I'd prayed,
  I'd trusted,
  but I'd anticipated the wrong thing,
  expecting you to act as I wanted
  instead of giving myself to your will.
Forgive me, Lord,
  and teach me to open my eyes to the unexpected,
  to the constant surprise of your love.
Amen.

Ponder

- What experiences have made you think again about the scope of God's purpose and the breadth of his love? Has God sometimes acted in unexpected ways in your life?
- Have you become set in your ways, your faith settled into a rut? Are you still open to the possibility of God surprising you?
- What factors might cause you to close your mind to the unexpected? How can you avoid this happening?

Close

Almighty God,
    teach me that whatever I know of you,
    there is far more that I do not,
    and that whatever I understand of your purpose,
    there is much that I haven't even begun to grasp.
Save me, then, from closing my mind to all you are doing
    and all you shall yet do.
In Christ's name I ask it.
Amen.

Day 2: Open to question

Approach

Gracious God,
   show me this day where I am faithful
   and where I am faithless,
   and equip me to honour you with my whole being.
Amen.

Read

Hear what God has to say, you rulers of Sodom! Pay attention to his instruction, you people of Gomorrah! Of what interest to me, says the Lord, are your never-ending sacrifices? I've had more than my fill of your burnt offerings of rams . . . I take no pleasure in the blood of oxen, rams or goats. Who asked you to bring such things to me in worship? I don't want you trampling over my courts any longer. Your offerings are a waste of time, and as for incense, I find it abhorrent. Frankly, I loathe and despise your pious get-togethers to celebrate the new moon, the Sabbath or other so-called sacred occasions, for they are tarnished by wickedness. I honestly have no interest in such festivals: they have worn me out, becoming nothing more than a weight around my neck. So, then, when you spread out your hands in prayer, I will hide my eyes from you; even if you offer many prayers, I will not listen. Your hands are full of blood; wash and make yourselves clean. Take your evil deeds out of my sight! Stop doing wrong, learn to do right! Seek justice, encourage the oppressed, defend the cause of the fatherless, plead the case of the widow.
Isaiah 1:10-17

Reflect

Are you open to the possibility that some of the opinions you hold might be wrong? Put as generally as that, the answer from almost all of us would probably be yes, but how far we are willing to admit the possibility of error will depend on the matter under consideration. We might, for example, be convinced (as I used to be) that commitment is spelt with two 't's or that 'privilege' is spelt 'privelege'. Few of us would refuse to accept our mistake in the face of an appropriate authority proving we are wrong. The most it would cost is a momentary loss of face. On other occasions, however, the situation is very different. If we've built our lives on a fundamental principle, or attempted to live according to certain moral precepts, then to have those challenged involves a major rethink that may have a significant impact on virtually every aspect of how we perceive ourselves and how we live. Facing up to questions can be costly, yet such questioning is essential if we are to grow as individuals and in our relationship with God. That truth emerges repeatedly in the Scriptures, and above all in the message of the prophets. Isaiah, Amos, Malachi and Hosea, to name but a few, passionately called their listeners to examine their lifestyles and ask searching questions of them. All right, says Isaiah, in the words of our reading, they claim to love God, but do their actions reinforce their words? They regularly offer worship, but do their deeds sing to the same tune as their song? They profess love of God, but is this love expressed through seeking his will and purpose, pursuing the same ends that he works towards? In other words, is their faith as real as they imagine, or are they living a lie?

Unsurprisingly, the response that greeted the prophets was frequently hostile. It hurts to face such intense scrutiny. Yet now, as then, we need to be open to just that if we are to stay true to our faith. It may be that nothing needs changing – that we are following Christ as faithfully today as the moment we first committed ourselves to his service. It may be that questions highlight strengths rather than weaknesses, commitment rather than faithlessness, growth rather than decline, but equally they may expose areas where our love has grown cold, our loyalties are divided, our commitment is compromised or our faith is weak. It's not easy to admit such things, still less to make the changes needed to put matters right, but if we fail to do so, what seems a minor malaise today might prove terminal to our faith tomorrow.

If we would make the most of Advent and respond to the challenges it brings, we need to ask first the fundamental question: Are we open to question?

Pray

Living God,
 I talk so glibly of justice for the poor,
 hope for the oppressed,
 fair shares for the exploited,
 but I rarely pause to ponder my part in their plight,
 my share of culpability for the ills of this world.
I speak of compassion for the sick,
 care for the lonely,
 support for the weak
 and love for the outcast,
 but my thoughts are focused firmly on self
 and my own small world.
It's easy to pray,
 so much harder to act;
 easy to question the actions of others,
 so much harder to question my own;
 yet whenever I act without considering the consequences
 or fail to respond from my plenty to those in need,
 I deny my words through deeds,
 my faith through actions,
 your love through *my* complacency.
Help me to examine my lifestyle and discipleship honestly,
 so that I may not simply talk of your concern for all,
 but show it
 in all that I am

and all that I do,
to the glory of your name.
Amen.

Ponder

- Are you open to the possibility that your discipleship is not all it should be? In what areas might it be weakest?
- When did you last pause to assess the depth of your discipleship? What yardsticks can it be measured against?
- Is your worship of God reinforced by service?

Close

Gracious God,
  where I am weak, show me;
  where I am complacent, challenge me;
  where I am faithless, rebuke me;
  where I am wrong, forgive me.
Grant me a mind to know you,
  a heart to love you,
  a spirit to serve you
  and a life to proclaim you,
  through Jesus Christ my Lord.
Amen.

Day 3: Open to God's guidance

Approach

Living Lord,
 I come seeking your guidance.
Reach out
 and lead me forward,
 in the way of Christ.
Amen.

Read

The sun will rise over us from heaven, to shine on those sitting in darkness and in the shadow of death, to guide our feet into the way of peace.
Luke 1:78-79

Reflect

What does it mean to be open to God's guidance? Does it mean receiving clear instructions concerning each decision we have to make, unmistakably hearing his voice at every moment of the day? Discipleship would be much easier if that were so, but in my experience things don't usually work that way. We may occasionally gain a strong sense that God is calling us to a particular task or challenging us on a specific issue, but such moments are the exception rather than the rule – wonderful when they come but not a commonplace experience. Most of the time it's more a matter of following *guidelines* rather than receiving specific *guidance*, but such guidelines are no less challenging or valuable. Whether through the words of the Bible, a sermon, a book or another Christian, God can and frequently does speak powerfully, challenging us concerning the people we are and the lives we lead. A passage on love, for example, might inspire us to more committed relationships and service; a verse on the needs of the poor might quicken our consciences and lead us to give more generously; a chapter on justice might cause us to question our lifestyle; and so we could go on. The crunch question, however, is whether we are open to such guidance. If only God did guide unequivocally, there would be no problem, for – assuming we count ourselves Christians – it would be well nigh impossible to ignore his voice. But when it comes to guidelines it's different. We can too easily simply close our Bibles or turn to another page. We can tell ourselves that we're doing our bit, or at least our best, and that a challenge therefore doesn't apply to us. We can question whether it's really God speaking or simply us reading too much into things. Or we can interpret words and ideas in ways that suit us best, making as few demands on us as possible.

To respond when we feel questioned, unsettled, challenged, threatened takes courage, yet it is the heart of real faith, perhaps explaining why God tends to offer guidelines more often than precise instructions, for directions served up on a plate would not be faith at all but blind obedience. Many of us will never receive a dramatic call, an unmistakable 'word of the Lord' telling us what we should do or where we should go, but God has a knack of speaking nonetheless, probing into the depth and sincerity of our discipleship, the quality of our love and the extent of our commitment, and, through that, if we are willing to hear and listen, he indeed offers guidance for each day. What then of you: are you open to guidance?

Pray

Living God,
    I recall today how you have guided your people across the years,
    leading them from earliest times.
I recall how you called Abraham to venture out into the unknown,
    Moses to lead your people out of Egypt,
    and Joshua to take them into the Promised Land;
    how you called kings to rule over them
    and judges and prophets to speak your word.

21

I recall how you called shepherds in the fields
   and wise men from the East
   to go to Bethlehem to see the Christ-child,
   how, in Christ, you chose twelve ordinary people to be disciples
   and how, on the Damascus Road,
   you called Paul to become Apostle to the Gentiles.
Equally, though, I recognise how you have spoken
   to countless others across the years,
   often calling less directly,
   but guiding just as surely:
   confronting through your word,
   inspiring through your love,
   enabling through your power,
   renewing through your grace.
Open my eyes in turn to all the ways you continue to prompt,
   my ears to the ways you speak,
   and my life to the way you guide,
   and help me to respond,
   in Jesus' name.
Amen.

Ponder

- In what ways have you been conscious of God's guiding over the years?

- Have there been times when you have resisted his guidance? Why did you resist, and how?

- Is there a danger sometimes of asking for clear and unmistakable guidance when God has shown you the path to take all along, if only you would look harder?

Close

Sovereign God,
  give me a sense of all you would have me be,
  and an understanding of the life you would have me live,
  and may that shape all I do and say and think,
  this and every day.
Amen.

Day 4: Open to others

Approach

Gracious God,
  grant me an open mind,
  a responsive heart
  and a receptive spirit,
  that I might hear your voice
  however you choose to speak.
Amen.

Read

As he reclined in the house, many tax collectors and sinners came and reclined with him at table. Seeing this, the Pharisees challenged his disciples, 'Why does your teacher eat with tax collectors and sinners?' Hearing this, Jesus responded, 'It is not the healthy who need a physician but those who are sick. Leave us alone and mark this: "I desire mercy rather than sacrifice, for I came not to call the righteous but sinners."'
Matthew 9:10-13

Reflect

How open are you to other people? No doubt we all like to think we are, but how true is that in practice? Are we open, for example, to the opinions of those who think differently to us? Are we open to people of other theological persuasions and doctrinal positions, to members of other faiths, to people whose tastes and lifestyles differ dramatically from our own? In reality, differences of outlook, belief and character all too easily estrange us from others so that we want little if anything to do with them. We don't consciously avoid those who are different – indeed we may be more than happy to pass the time of day with them, exchanging social pleasantries – but there is no contact at a deeper level, no meaningful dialogue or meeting of minds. We are effectively closed to the possibility of their world having anything to say to ours, still less of God confronting us through them.

The same was true in the time of Jesus, perhaps yet more so. Gentiles had little place in the life of Jews, unless they were willing to adopt Jewish customs, ritual and belief to the letter of the law. Women had little status in a world of men, regarded more as possessions than individuals. Lepers were treated as outcasts, tax collectors as traitors, prostitutes and adulterers as fit only to be stoned, the sick as those being punished for sin, and so we could go on. Yet these, of course, feature large in the gospel as those who responded to God's love in Christ and whose lives testified to his redemptive purpose. It is no accident that God chose an insignificant girl to bring Christ into the world and a humble carpenter from Nazareth to be her partner; that he chose shepherds to hear the good news first; that he led magi from the East – in other words, Gentiles – to be among the first to respond; that Jesus called a tax collector as one of his twelve; that he mixed repeatedly throughout his ministry with those dismissed as unclean or unworthy; and that he laid hands on the sick whenever and wherever the opportunity arose. Here, if ever, was the man for others, and here also we see the one who calls us to look beyond the social, religious, cultural or racial barriers we erect, recognising that God speaks time and again through those we least expect.

In an increasingly divided world we need to hear that message more than ever. In a predominantly insular society we need urgently to reflect on what that challenge means. In a Church still riven by division, if more today in terms of worship and theology than denominational differences, we need to consider what God is saying to us. Whoever we are, we need to ask whether we're as open to others as we like to think we are, and as open as God would have us be.

Pray

Sovereign God,
    I call you Lord of all,
    but my life doesn't match my words,
    for I'm turned in on my own small world,
    hostile to new ideas,
    suspicious of anything different,
    closed to all but the few.
I preach openness,
    of the need to see beyond the barriers we erect,
    but they are still there deep within,
    prejudices and expectations that I scarcely recognise,
    let alone combat.
Unconsciously, I set boundaries on those you might use,
    those you might speak through,
    even those who might respond to your love,
    assuming your thoughts to be my thoughts,
    your ways the same as my own.
Forgive me, Lord.
Forgive me for failing to see you in others
    because I've refused to look,
    for failing to hear you because I've refused to listen.
Forgive the limits I've set on your power
    and the fetters I've placed on your grace,
    setting myself up as judge and jury
    when in fact the verdict concerns me.
Open my eyes to the contribution others can make to my life –
    to the insights they can share,
    the gifts they can exercise,
    the lessons they can teach
    and the example they can give.
Open my mind to the way you can work
    through those I least expect –
    speaking your word,
    revealing your power,
    displaying your love,

fulfilling your will.
Open my heart to others
as you have so freely opened yours to me,
and so may I truly call you Lord of all.
Amen.

Ponder

- Do unrecognised prejudices still have a hold in your life, shaping your attitude towards certain people or groups in society? Are you open to the possibility that God might speak to you through such people?
- How ready are you to listen to points of view other than your own? When did you last attempt to do so?
- Why do we close our minds to some people? What sort of factors lie behind this? Can you discern such factors at work in your life?

Close

Lord of all,
open my heart to others
and to all you would say through them,
and so open my heart to you
and to your life-giving word.
In Christ's name I ask it.
Amen.

Day 5: Open to the present

Approach

Sovereign God,
  teach me your way and show me your will,
  that I may live and work for you now,
  to the glory of your name.
Amen.

Read

He said to them, 'When you pray, use words like these: "Our Father in heaven, to you be praise and honour. May your kingdom come and your will be done, on earth as it is in heaven."'
Matthew 6:9-10

Reflect

In 1844 Karl Marx delivered his infamous and damning appraisal of Christianity as 'the opium of the people'. In his view, religion's appeal to another dimension of reality, and, in particular, to an afterlife in which the evils of this world will be rectified, blinds people to the reality of life now and the response this demands from us. Many of his theories have subsequently been discredited, but in one thing at least he was right: faith can obscure our responsibilities in the present. Many Christians in Europe, for example, decided that the horrors of the Holocaust during the Second World War were none of their concern. Christian commitment was reduced to a matter of personal devotion, its social implications ignored. Similarly, some Christians today maintain that the gospel has nothing to say on political, economic or ecological issues, such matters being of worldly rather than spiritual significance. It is hard to understand, however, how anyone can hold such views in the light of the teaching of Jesus, and, in particular, the words of the prayer he taught his disciples. 'May your kingdom come and your will be done, *on earth as it is in heaven.'* The last part of the sentence is as important as the first. God's kingdom is not limited to the future but begins here and now. It is something we are called to pray and work for, to help make real on earth through our life and witness.

How, then, do *we* see God's kingdom? Do we understand it as confined to the distant future, far removed from life as we know it, or are we open to it taking shape around us? Do we regard it as dependent solely on God's sovereign activity, or do we believe we have a part to play in furthering its growth? We cannot afford to divorce faith from daily life because the world is precious in God's eyes, his purpose extending to all people at all times. It is up to each of us to do what we can to bring God's kingdom closer here on earth. Only then can we pray the Lord's Prayer, and mean it.

Pray

Lord,
    I pray often that your will may be done
    and your kingdom come,
    but I rarely stop to consider what that involves.
It's something I ask of *you*,
    expecting *you* to accomplish it,
    you to do the spadework,
    forgetting that you need people like *me* to be your hands and feet,
    your agents within the world,
    proclaiming the gospel,
    sharing your love,
    offering our service.
Forgive me, Lord, for abdicating my share of the responsibility;
    for seeing the kingdom solely as some future paradise,
    and so ignoring the hell that some endure today.
Teach me to reach out in the name of Christ,
    and through my life and witness
    to contribute something meaningful to your purpose,

so that a glimpse of heaven may shine through on earth,
to your praise and glory.
Amen.

Ponder

- Do you see the kingdom of God as something that will come in the distant future or as having already begun here on earth?
- In what ways do you see people working today to further the growth of that kingdom and to make it more real here and now?
- What are you doing to help bring God's kingdom closer? When you pray 'Your kingdom come, on earth as it is in heaven', do you mean it?

Close

Loving God,
    open my eyes to see you,
    my ears to hear you,
    my heart to love you
    and my life to serve you.
So may I share in the work of your kingdom
    and the fulfilment of your will,
    to the glory of your name.
Amen.

Day 6: Open to the best

Approach

Almighty God,
   though so much troubles and confuses,
   reveal to me more fully the wonder of your love
   that gives meaning to life,
   and hope, now and always.
Amen.

Read

We know that all things work together for good with those who love God, who have been called according to his purpose . . . I am convinced that nothing can separate us from Christ's love. Neither death nor life, nor angels nor demons, nor the present nor the future, nor any powers, nor height nor depth nor anything else in all creation, will ever be able to separate us from the love of God that is ours in Christ Jesus our Lord.
Romans 8:28, 38-39

Reflect

'Hope for the best; prepare for the worst' – that, for me, sums up the way we need to approach life. We need to be realistic about the bad things that might happen, and do our best to ensure we can cope should they do so, but we need also to be positive in out-look, always searching for the good rather than the bad, seeing opportunities rather than obstacles, and focusing on joys rather than sorrows. Many will say this is simply naivety, and if we only had this life to go on they'd probably be right. Anyone whose experience is overshadowed by sickness, sorrow or suffering will find it hard, if not impossible, to hope for the best in terms of what life might bring, since it has already in many ways confirmed their fears for the worst. The gospel, however, gives a new dimension to hope through its promise of an eternal kingdom and everlasting blessing. That surely is what Paul was driving at in his words to the Romans. In terms of our daily experience, things patently do not always work together for good: we need only think of Christians who have died for their faith over the years, or those who have wasted away due to terminal illness, or whose loved ones have been killed, to find powerful confirmation that this is so. Yet, as Paul says later in the same chapter (Romans 8:38-39), nothing in heaven or earth, in this life or the next, will ever be able to separate us from the love of God which is ours in Christ.

Advent calls us to prepare for the worst in that it counsels us to examine our lifestyles, to consider our discipleship, and to reflect on who and what we are, gauging whether we have responded from the heart to the challenge of the good news. Yet it calls us also, not simply to *hope* for the best but to *expect* it, confident that having responded, and despite the fact that we still repeatedly fail to follow Christ as faithfully as we would like, all things *will* ultimately work together for good with those who love him.

Pray

Mighty God,
  you promise that for those who love you
  all things will work together for good,
  but it's not always easy to believe that
  in the traumas and turmoil of life.
We face so much that seems to deny your love
  and frustrate your will,
  our world scarred by suffering and sorrow,
  evil and injustice,
  that leave few of us untouched.
All too often hopes are dashed and dreams broken
  by the icy blast of reality,
  so that, though we still speak of your purpose for our lives,
  it becomes hard to see how your hand might be at work,

weaving the tangled and broken threads of our daily experience
into a rich and meaningful tapestry.
Reach out, O God, and restore our vision.
Teach us to see beyond the here and now to your eternity,
beyond present pain to future blessing,
beyond current despair to promised jubilation.
Help us to recognise that though life now may make no sense,
all will one day become clear;
that though evil seems triumphant,
good will finally prevail.
In the name of Christ we ask it.
Amen.

Ponder

- How far do you think it is possible to speak of things working together for good in this life? What experiences shape your answer?

- What personal experiences or issues in the lives of others make it hard to speak of things working together for good?

- Looking back on life, are there ways in which things worked together for good even though it didn't seem like it at the time?

Close

Gracious God,
teach me to live every moment of every day
in the light of the eternal tomorrow you hold in store
for me and all your people,
through Jesus Christ my Lord.
Amen.

Day 7: Open to better still

Approach

Sovereign God,
    open my heart each day to the joys you so freely give,
    but teach me also that these are but a foretaste
    of all that is yet to come,
    by the grace of Christ.
Amen.

Read

No eye has seen, nor ear heard, nor any heart conceived of the things that God has prepared for those who love him.
1 Corinthians 2:9

Reflect

What is better than the best? Strictly speaking, of course, the answer is nothing; 'best' by definition means better than anything else. In practice, however, the term is always qualified, taken to mean 'the best so far'. An athlete, for example, sets a new world record, the best-ever time up to that point, but no one expects that record never to be broken. It is there to be beaten, the yardstick against which all athletes will measure their performances from that point on until a new best-ever is established. A student may achieve the highest set of A grades ever recorded in a particular school, but that does not mean another student will not one day surpass this. So we could go on in just about every field of human endeavour we might care to mention. And so it is that we wish someone 'the *very* best of luck', recognising that our conception of 'best' rarely goes far enough.

If that's true of everyday life it's all the more so when it comes to considering our ultimate destiny. We looked yesterday at the need to hope for the best but whatever we conceive that 'best' to

34

be we can be sure we have barely begun to grasp the full wonder of what it involves. Any language we use to talk of the things of God, as with talk concerning God himself, is necessarily flawed since we are attempting to describe the indescribable, to put into finite concepts realities that finally go beyond this world. I've tried many times to get my head round the idea of eternity. I've struggled to explain the idea of heaven to my children when they've talked to me about death. I've debated with other Christians what sort of place it might be and what kind of life we might live there, but each time I have eventually had to admit defeat. Why? Because, as the Apostle Paul so eloquently reminds us, 'No eye has seen, nor ear heard, nor any heart conceived of the things that God has prepared for those who love him' (1 Corinthians 2:9).

Remember those words this Advent. Remember them always. As Christians we do not simply hope for the best, we do not simply expect the best; we look forward to a kingdom and a blessing that is better than anything we can ever ask or imagine – to an experience in eternity that nothing can ever hope to surpass – one which, alone, we can truly call 'the best'.

Pray

Loving God,
>   I try to picture what heaven is like,
>   but words fail me.
>   I try to imagine a world of everlasting bliss,
>   but it defies my limited reach of mind.
>   I try to comprehend the wonder of your presence,
>   but it is beyond me.
>   I try to envisage the blessings you hold in store,
>   but I barely know where to start.
>   Teach me,
>   though I cannot fully understand,
>   to continue trusting in your purpose,
>   looking forward in eager anticipation
>   to the dawn of your kingdom.

Teach me, above all,
   to keep the vision alive,
   confident that however wonderful
   I may conceive your kingdom to be,
   however rich in blessing and brimming over with joy,
   the reality you hold in store is more special,
   more breathtaking,
   than anything I can ever ask or hope for –
   a treasure beyond price.
Amen.

Ponder

- How do you picture heaven? What does the prospect of eternal life in God's kingdom actually mean to you?
- Does a difficulty in imagining what heaven might be like trouble you at all? Does it detract in any way from the resurrection hope God has given in Christ?
- Is there a danger of trying too hard to define the exact nature of heaven? Does it make sense to attempt any such a definition, given that we are talking about the things of God?

Close

Almighty God,
   though the details remain a mystery,
   defying human comprehension,
   teach me, in the light of the joy you give now,
   to trust you for eternity,
   secure in the knowledge of your love that will never fail.
Amen.

Second week of Advent

A time to prepare

The week ahead

The traditional emphasis in the second week of Advent is on the importance of being prepared to welcome Jesus, both here and now into our lives and on his final return. The classic symbol of this is John the Baptist, who is portrayed even before his birth as the one sent to prepare the way of the Lord, and who later calls people to repentance in readiness to welcome the Messiah. The irony, of course, is that, despite the long years of expecting and waiting, many were not ready to receive him when he came, and the lesson drawn from this is that we too may not be as ready as we like to think we are.

In what ways then should we be prepared? What does being ready involve in practice? I want to focus this week on various possibilities: a readiness to say sorry, to *be* sorry, to grow in faith, to live life to the full, to give to others and to receive God's grace. There are, of course, many other aspects of faith that are equally important but these take us to the heart of discipleship. Get them right and we will find ourselves prepared for anything; ready not only to serve Christ now but also joyfully to greet him when he comes again.

Day 1: Prepared to say sorry

Approach

Sovereign God,
   in your awesome grace receive me as I am,
   and by your redeeming power direct what I shall be,
   through Christ,
   my Lord and Saviour.
Amen.

Read

If we claim to have no sin, we are fooling ourselves and the truth has no place in us. If we confess our sins, God is just, and we can rely on him to forgive our sins and cleanse us from all evil.
1 John 1:8-9

Reflect

'Anyone who makes a mistake and fails to acknowledge it, commits another' – so run the wise words of the Chinese philosopher Confucius. Most of us will recognise the truth of that observation but nonetheless struggle when it comes to acting upon it, for few things are harder than admitting we're wrong. We find it embarrassing, even humiliating, to admit to fallibility, so we attempt to gloss over, excuse or deny our errors. Occasionally, we might save face through doing so, but equally often we end up digging ourselves into a pit from which it is increasingly difficult to escape. Of course, some mistakes are harder to acknowledge than others. Owning up to some minor slip-up is one thing; acknowledging a fundamental weakness or flaw in our character is quite another. The more something touches on who and what we perceive ourselves to be, the harder it becomes to be honest and objective. Yet it is precisely here that honesty is vital if we are to avoid living a lie and denying ourselves true peace of mind and fulfilment.

At the heart of Advent is God's promise of forgiveness and new life to those who acknowledge their faults. This means more though than simply offering vague confession – anyone can do that, but it doesn't get us very far. True confession means taking a long hard look at ourselves and acknowledging where our life might be found wanting. It means listening to God's challenge, from wherever it might come, and being open to having our comfortable preconceptions and assumptions challenged. Such a searching examination can be hugely painful, but it is also the pathway to inner healing and wholeness, to a peace beyond human understanding, to new life in Christ. Are you ready to face up to everything that is wrong in your life, and to acknowledge it, humbly and honestly, before God?

Pray

I prayed, Lord,
    asking forgiveness for all that is wrong in my life,
    all the ways I fail you,
    and I thought that was an end to it:
    that I'd made my confession and received your forgiveness.
To a point I was right,
    for you *had* forgiven –
    gladly,
    freely,
    wholeheartedly –
    yet there were so many faults that I hadn't brought,
    hadn't even begun to acknowledge,
    and much as you longed to release me from those too,
    you couldn't touch them –
    couldn't bring me the healing, wholeness,
    renewal and restoration you so yearned for me to enjoy.
They will imprison me still –
    denying,
    destroying –
    until I recognise their presence,
    and bring them before you,

for only then can you draw their poison,
cleanse the wounds
and heal the scars.
Forgive me, Lord, for having taken the easy way –
acknowledging general wrongdoing rather than specific errors,
offering sweeping confession rather than genuine remorse.
Forgive me for confusing a vague acknowledgement of guilt
with a searching and sincere identification of my weaknesses.
Give me honesty and humility to recognise my faults,
and to confess them with genuine sorrow,
so that I may receive your healing, renewing touch,
through Jesus Christ my Lord.
Amen.

Ponder

- How often do you make time in your prayers for confession?
What do you see as the purpose of such prayers? Are they for
God's benefit or ours?

- Are your prayers of confession specific – identifying particular
weaknesses, mistakes and failings – or general? Does a blanket
confession ('Lord, forgive me all that is wrong in my life')
achieve anything? Does being more specific achieve more?

- Are there things wrong in your life that you need to face up to?
Have you avoided confessing them because you would rather
not meet that challenge?

Close

Merciful God,
teach me to recognise my faults
and to acknowledge them candidly to you,
so that I may find forgiveness,
and be touched by the renewing and restoring grace of Christ,
in whose name I pray.
Amen.

Day 2: Prepared to *be* sorry

Approach

Lord Jesus Christ,
　help me so to know and love you
　that my words and deeds may be one,
　just as everything *you* said and did testified to who you were
　and continues to speak today.
Amen. ⟨

Read

John the Baptist appeared during that time in the wilderness of Judea, with the message, 'Turn from your sinful ways, for the kingdom of heaven is dawning.' People flocked to him from Jerusalem, Judea and the entire length of the River Jordan, in which he baptised them as they made confession of their sins.
Matthew 3:1, 5-6

Reflect

It's often noted that sorry is the hardest word to say, few of us relishing the prospect of acknowledging our mistakes, yet if *saying* sorry is difficult, *being* sorry is harder still. However awkward it may be to spit them out, words don't actually cost us very much; indeed, by themselves they can be relatively meaningless. Even when they express genuine remorse, words alone are not enough unless they are reinforced by actions. If I say sorry for doing something wrong and then straightaway go and do it again, my words lose credibility. If I apologise for acting or speaking in a way that caused hurt, only to do precisely the same thing afterwards, the sincerity of my apology will inevitably be called into question. Being sorry means wanting and trying to change, doing one's best to avoid making the same mistake again. We may not always succeed in that, some weaknesses, habits and failings proving harder to overcome than others, but it should at least be evident that we are doing our best to put right in our lives those things that we know to be wrong.

Is that true of you? When you apologise for something – an unkind word, a foolish action, a careless mistake – do you strive to ensure that it never happens again? When you offer confession to God, do you do so resolved to try harder to conquer temptation when it comes next time, to overcome that weakness of yours that caused you to fall, to follow Christ more faithfully in the days ahead? In other words, whenever you say sorry, are you prepared also to *be* sorry?

Pray

I still haven't learned, Lord, have I?
I've made progress –
    a little anyway –
    recognising and confessing my faults,
    but that's about as far as it goes.
Though I've *said* sorry,
    I've not actually *shown* it –
    either to you or to others –
    and, to my shame, I've scarcely even tried.
I thought words were all it took,
    one simply expression of regret sufficient to put things right,
    but I realise now that pious sentiments are not enough –
    exposed as hollow,
    empty,
    meaningless,
    unless there's something more solid to back them up;
    some attempt to mend my ways,
    live differently,
    correct what I know to be wrong.
I may not succeed in that –
    not even get anywhere close –

45

but unless I at least attempt to change
I can say sorry as often as I like
and few will take notice,
for though my lips will say one thing
my life will profess another.
Teach me, then, not just to confess my faults
but also to strive, as far as it lies within me, to overcome them;
to express remorse not just in words but in deeds.
Teach me to *be* sorry,
in the name of Christ.
Amen.

Ponder

- Is it possible to be sorry about something if you do not attempt to put it right?

- Are there things you know to be wrong in your life that you confess but do nothing about? What does this say about your confession? Are you deceiving yourself? Do you imagine God can be deceived?

- Do you agree that a genuine desire to amend one's ways is more important than succeeding in doing so? Do you sometimes use this as an excuse not to change, or do you make the opposite mistake of being excessively hard on yourself when you fall short?

Close

Gracious God,
come and work within me as you will,
not just today but every day,
until you have finished your new creation
and my whole being proclaims your glory.
Amen.

Day 3: Prepared to grow

Approach

Sovereign God,
  take the seeds of faith you have sown within me.
Feed them,
  nurture them,
  and bring from them a rich harvest,
  to the glory of your name.
Amen.

Read

He gave some to be apostles, some prophets, some evangelists, and some pastors and teachers, to prepare God's people for practical service and to build up the body of Christ, so that we will be united in faith and in the knowledge of the Son of God, attaining a maturity that corresponds to the full measure we see in Christ. Then we will no longer be like children, blown here and there on every doctrinal breeze, carried along by ingenious but ultimately flawed human arguments. Instead, speaking the truth in love, we will in every respect grow into the one who is the Head; that is, Christ, in whom the whole body is assembled and held together by the ligaments he supplies for it, and through whom each part is able to function as it should so that the body can grow as it builds itself up in love.
Ephesians 4:11-16

Reflect

It's funny, isn't it, how when we're young everyone over a certain age seems not just grown-up but positively old? Even a 20-year-old seems hugely mature to a child, accorded a corresponding breadth of experience and understanding that may bear little or no relation to reality. It comes as a shock, as the years go by, to realise that though we change in some ways we remain essentially the same person beneath the surface. Experience brings wisdom and maturity of sorts, but that does not mean that a whole and integrated personality develops automatically; indeed, for some it never develops at all.

Similarly, maturity in Christ should not be taken for granted. We cannot sit back and assume it will take care of itself, nor should we imagine that it arises routinely as a direct consequence of the years we've been a Christian. If we are to grow in faith, we need, first, the desire to do so and, second, the resolve to help it happen. We cannot achieve that solely through our own efforts, however laudable our intentions. We depend on Christ for nourishment and nurture, encouragement and inspiration, succour and strength, and without him faith is doomed to wither and die. But, in turn, he needs our cooperation: our willingness to make time for quiet reflection and devotion, our willingness to listen and learn, our hunger and thirst for righteousness. Christian discipleship is not just about a one-off act of commitment but about an ongoing relationship, an unfolding story, a continuing process of growth.

Is that how we see our faith? Are we still eager to grow towards maturity in Christ: to love him more deeply, serve him more faithfully, honour him more truly and know him more fully? Do we yearn to enlarge our understanding of his purpose, enrich our experience of his grace and advance the cause of his kingdom? Or are we content simply to drift along, our horizons the same tomorrow as they are today? To do that is to deny ourselves the riches God wants us to enjoy, settling for the moon rather than the stars. It is also to deny *him*: to deprive him of the relationship he would share with us, and the service we could offer. He wants us to grow up in faith, shaped in the image of Christ; to become a little more like him day by day. Don't pass that opportunity by.

Pray

I still used the right language, Lord,
 still talked of growing in grace,
 bearing fruit,
 attaining maturity in Christ,
 but the facts spoke otherwise –
 my discipleship not just standing still
 but in danger of terminal decline.
It wasn't meant to happen, of course,
 but I'd grown careless,
 complacent,
 forgetting that faith needs to be nourished and nurtured
 if it is not to shrivel up and die.
Thankfully, you called me back,
 renewing as you have done so many times before;
 my appetite restoring –
 and bringing a hunger to know you better,
 to explore the breadth, length,
 height and depth of your love in Christ –
 but I'd been close to losing faith,
 to falling away . . .
 too close!
Forgive me, Lord, for being content simply to drift along.
Forgive my casualness in discipleship
 and complacency in worship;
 my leaving everything to you as if I've no part to play.
Teach me that however much I have understood of your greatness
 or experienced of your love,
 I have barely begun to explore the whole,
 and so help me grow not just today but every day,
 to the glory of your name.
Amen.

Ponder

- What factors might cause your faith to stop growing? How far are these present in your life?

- Is your faith growing as it once did? Do you still expect to learn and experience more of the love of God in Christ?

- What steps are you taking to ensure that your faith does not stand still? Is it time you did something more?

Close

Living God,
   create in me a thirst to know you better,
   a hunger to grow in grace
   and a yearning to mature in discipleship.
Prompt, guide and instruct through your Spirit,
   and so deepen my faith a little more each day,
   to your praise and glory.
Amen.

Day 4: Prepared to live

Approach

Living God,
  touch this day with your presence,
  this moment with your love.
Speak to me that I may speak for you,
  live in me that I may live for you,
  through Jesus Christ my Lord.
Amen.

Read

I have come so that you might have life, and live it to the full.
John 10:10b

Reflect

'Get a life!' When, I wonder, did you last hear that expression used? We hear it so often today it's in danger of becoming a cliché. So what does it mean? Frequently, it's little more than a cheap jibe, a way of belittling those whose tastes and interests differ from our own, but, properly used, it presents a challenge to those who have become so wrapped up in a particular concern – whether it be a hobby, relationship, job or whatever – that they have no time for anything else. In other words, the phrase is a call to a more rounded existence, a balanced lifestyle that makes time for the innumerable gifts each day has to offer – work and rest, study and play, serious-ness and laughter, to name but a few.

  If anyone should be able to issue such a challenge it is surely those who profess the name of Christ, for at the heart of faith is his promise of life in all its fullness, but is that what we see in practice? In some cases, happily, yes, but by no means always. All too easily we can substitute the abundant life Jesus offers for a pale imitation,

51

confusing faith with religion and church with discipleship. For example, I have seen some Christians, good and committed people, sucked so deeply into the life of a fellowship that there is little room for anything else, just about every moment of their free time dominated by a cycle of meetings, duties and responsibilities. I have seen others effectively drawing away from the world, shutting out what they see as pagan influences that might lead them or their families astray. Others again wash their hands of this life in a different sense, claiming that we should not concern ourselves with social and environmental issues but focus instead on the life to come. Is this 'life in all its fullness'? Not for me, it isn't! I can understand where such people are coming from, but, as I see it, if faith becomes a denial rather than affirmation of life something is seriously wrong. Of course, not everything in this world is good – far from it – so, yes, we do need to exercise discernment and to know where to draw the line. But we need also to recognise the good in life – the special and beautiful, everything that has the capacity to fascinate, inspire, challenge, thrill and bless – recognising and receiving it as God's gift. That, surely, is the challenge of Christian discipleship: not to keep the world at arms' length but to live within it in a way that honours God, celebrating the best and avoiding the worst, building on the good and challenging the bad. Ultimate fulfilment is indeed yet to come, life possessing a dimension that is only realised beyond the grave, but every moment God gives is a foretaste of joys yet in store, to be welcomed and celebrated. As the Psalmist reminds us (118:24): 'This is the day that the Lord has made; let us rejoice and be glad in it' (NRSV).

Pray

It sounds so wonderful, Lord,
    so rich and replete with promise:
    life in all its fullness –
    abundant,
    overflowing.
But do I live in such a way as to show that,

in a way that makes people sit up and take notice,
    desiring such life for themselves?
Is each day a celebration of your goodness,
    each moment a joyful response to the blessings
    you so freely bestow?
Or do people see in me instead a denial of life,
    a taking refuge in creed and doctrine, religion and ritual,
    retreating into the safe environment of church and fellowship,
    rather than embracing all that is good in your world,
    the inestimable treasures it has to offer?
It's not easy striking the right balance,
    for neither life nor this world are all good –
    not by a long way –
    so much bringing pain and sorrow,
    tarnished by evil,
    spoiled by sin.
Yet life is still your gift,
    fashioned by your hand and bearing your stamp;
    a bequest to be savoured,
    sanctified,
    celebrated.
Teach me, then, Lord, to live within this world
    yet not be conformed to it;
    to affirm the best and challenge the worst,
    living each day,
    each moment,
    in joyful thanksgiving.
Teach me to anticipate your promise of life to come
    by consecrating life *now*
    and living it to your praise and glory.
In Christ's name I pray.
Amen.

Ponder

- Is there a danger of becoming so sucked into church life that we effectively turn our backs on many of the good things this world has to offer? Can we become so heavenly-minded that we are of little earthly use? How far might this be said of your life?
- When Jesus spoke of life in all its fullness, was he referring simply to life after death or also to life now?
- Do you see life as a celebration? In what way has faith in Christ made it fuller for you?

Close

Gracious Lord,
    help me to build on the past
    and work for the future
    by living faithfully in the present,
    celebrating here and now your gift of life
    and consecrating myself afresh each day to your service.
In Christ's name I ask it.
Amen.

Day 5: Prepared to give

Approach

Lord Jesus Christ,
  whatever I offer to you,
  it can never surpass what you have given to me.
Teach me, then, to consecrate my time,
  my money,
  my gifts,
  my all,
  to your service
  and to your glory.
Amen.

Read

Let us never tire of doing what is right, for we will harvest a
reward in due season provided we do not lose heart. Whenever
an opportunity presents itself, then, let us strive for the welfare of
all, particularly those who belong to the family of faith.
Galatians 6:9-10

Reflect

'It is more blessed to give than receive', or so the saying goes, but
who actually first made such a claim? According to the Apostle
Paul, it was none other than Jesus, and that raises an interesting
question, because for some reason none of the four Gospels
mentions these words. I wonder why. Could it be the Evangelists
forgot them? I doubt it. Did they consider them unimportant? I
doubt that still more. Perhaps, then, they weren't present when
Jesus made this observation, but that seems unlikely in the extreme,
for how would Paul, who had never met Jesus in the flesh, know
of this saying if those who had followed him throughout the three

55

years of his earthly ministry apparently had never heard of it? The truth is we cannot account for the omission. Perhaps the Gospel writers simply assumed these words of Jesus went without saying, everything in his life and ministry making the point as words never could, but I wonder if, just possibly, they were reluctant at some deep subconscious level to spell things out, all too aware of the discomfiting challenge the words bring. You see, it's easy enough to say them, but infinitely harder to put them into practice. We'll succeed sometimes, of course. Which of us, for example, hasn't experienced the joy of bestowing gifts on a loved one or of watching children eagerly opening presents? We've probably equally found pleasure in giving to a good cause, it being heart-warming to feel we have helped to make a difference, no matter how small, to those in need. Yet for most of us, myself included, giving is strictly limited, its boundaries drawn up well within what we can afford, typically restricted to our small change. To give sacrificially, so that we go without, rarely enters the equation.

Contrast that with the example of Jesus. He came expressly to give, laying down his life so that we might share it, sacrificing everything that we might enjoy life in all its fullness. He doesn't demand, or even expect, that we give anything in return, but he invites us freely to respond, to share in the privilege of giving not as a duty but as a joy, whether it be our time, energy, love, service, money, possessions, talents or experience. No matter who we are, we all have something to give, something to share, something to contribute to others. The question is: do we do anything about it?

Pray

I'm good at giving, Lord . . .
    in theory.
I thought, only the other day, how wonderful it would be
    to make a difference:
    to bring hope to the poor,
    food to the hungry,
    medicine to the sick

and shelter to the homeless,
and I resolved, as soon as the bank balance could stand it,
to do something to make it happen –
to give, and give generously.
I thought of other things besides money –
of giving my time to write to someone, ring them, visit;
my skills to help others, serve the Church,
contribute towards the community;
my energy to share someone's load, support a cause,
advance the growth of your kingdom –
only each remained just a thought,
a good intention,
time somehow always too short,
skills already called on,
energies turned inwards rather than outwards.
Forgive me, Lord,
for I've not just deprived others but myself too,
each one of us the loser.
I intended much, but achieved little,
saw the need but failed to respond,
so wrapped up in self that what I thought I possessed
now in fact possesses me.
Teach me to recognise the joy of giving,
the privilege of sharing,
the fulfilment that comes through letting go,
and so help me, in my own small way,
to offer something to others,
in grateful response for all you have offered to me.
Amen.

Ponder

- What factors in life hold you back from giving as generously as you might?
- Have there been opportunities to give that you have spurned recently? Is your giving to God and to others in any way sacrificial?
- What can you do today to contribute something to others?

Close

Lord of all,
  inspire me,
  through all you have so freely given
  and all you continue each day to give,
  to respond in kind,
  giving generously to others,
  in the name of Christ.
Amen.

Day 6: Prepared to receive

Approach

Caring God,
  instead of striving to earn your love or to deserve your goodness,
  teach me simply to open my heart to your overflowing grace
  and to receive the love you so freely give.
In Christ's name I ask it.
Amen.

Read

God demonstrated his love like this – he sent his only Son into the world in order that we might live through him. In this is love, not that we loved God but that he loved us and sent his Son to be the expiation for our sins . . . He was in the world, and the world owed its existence to him, yet the world did not recognise him. He became part of what was his own, and his own people did not accept him. To all, though, who are ready to receive him and believe in his name, he gave the right to become God's children – children born not of blood or any union of the flesh, nor of any human desire, but of God.
1 John 4:9-10; John 1:10-13

Reflect

'You're too kind!' 'I couldn't possibly accept!' No doubt we've all received protests like those when we've offered someone a gift, and we've probably used similar words when a gift has been offered to us. But do we mean it? Is our refusal real? Often probably not, the words simply a polite if somewhat embarrassed way of expressing gratitude, but on occasions we genuinely find it hard to accept a gift, either because we feel undeserving of such largesse or because we are left stunned by its magnitude. If it is more blessed to give than to receive, it can correspondingly be harder to receive than to give. Perhaps that's why we struggle sometimes to accept the simple message at the heart of the gospel: the gift of God's Son, and of new life through him. 'Wonderful,' we say, 'what do I have to do to receive it? What does God ask of me in return? After all, we don't get something for nothing – everyone knows that – so what's the deal?' It's a natural way to think, and, despite our talk of grace and love, it's the way we all too often *do* think. We simply cannot help feeling that we must *do* something to earn God's forgiveness, merit his blessing, deserve his goodness; the idea of a free gift just does not fit in with our understanding of the world. 'Where's the catch?' we ask ourselves. 'Read the small print.'

Sadly, Christians have all too often been guilty of inserting small print of their own. You must believe this doctrine, this tenet of belief, claim some; otherwise you're not a Christian. You must belong to this church, that church, *any* church, or else your faith isn't real. You must exhibit particular gifts, distinctive manifesta-tions of the Spirit, or you've not been born again. You must adhere to certain principles, conform to moral guidelines, or you're beyond the pale. There may be much to commend the doctrines, churches, gifts and principles in questions, but these are nonetheless *our* requirements, not God's, and if we elevate them to the status of conditions for becoming a Christian we are not only misguided but also wrong. Unpalatable though some may find it, the message of the gospel is that God's love has no hidden clauses; it is there for the taking, extended to all, needing only our willingness to reach out and receive it.

Don't, then, set impossible standards for others, or for yourself. Don't labour under a burden of guilt, fretting that your faults might cause God to reject you. Don't measure yourself against some arbitrary yardstick of perfection that you feel you must live up to if you are to retain his favour. More than anything, the gospel is about God's free and unconditional love. Yes, of course he hopes this will make a difference to who and what we are, equipping, enabling and inspiring us to live as his people, but that is not a condition but a consequence of his love. He loved us before we ever loved him, and when we open our hearts to Christ, however flawed that response may be, we open a conduit for that love to pour through; one that will stay open unless we consciously close it. The gift is for you, for me, for everyone. Have you received it?

Pray

Amazing grace –
    that's what we speak of, Lord,
    that's what we claim for you:
    a gift offered to us freely,
    no strings attached,
    no price to pay.
It sounds wonderful,
    except that we don't really believe it,
    our lives making that all too clear,
    whatever our words may say.
You love us, we imagine,
    so long as we go to church,
    say our prayers,
    read your word.
You accept us
    so long as we believe the accepted dogma,
    recite the established creed,
    conform to the particular statement of faith.
You forgive us
    so long as we're essentially honest,
    decent,
    respectable –
    the sort of people you'd care to mix with.
You bless us, in other words, so long as we bless you,
    ready to scratch our backs provided we scratch yours first;
    your goodness conditional on our doing,
    believing and being the right thing.

We don't say it, of course,
 but we think it,
 or others tell us it's what we should think,
 and so gift becomes graft,
 joy becomes duty,
 what should be ours to receive becoming instead ours to earn.
Lord,
 forgive us for imposing *our* ways on you,
 our values and expectations.
Forgive us for limiting your love
 to the pale imitation we struggle to show to you and to others.
Above all, though,
 thank you for continuing to reach out to us each day,
 accepting us despite our getting it wrong,
 devoted to us despite our lack of devotion to you,
 loving us with your awesome, amazing grace!
Amen.

Ponder

- Do you find it hard to receive sometimes? What is the hardest thing about being the recipient of undeserved generosity?

- Do you find it hard to believe that God can truly forgive you? Do you still carry with you a sense of guilt for past faults and failings?

- Do you still labour under a sense of needing to earn your salvation and deserve God's goodness? Have you fully understood the meaning of 'grace'?

Close

Gracious God,
    teach me that you are more loving,
    more caring,
    more generous
    and more forgiving
    than I can ever dream possible,
    and so, instead of striving to earn your blessing,
    may I simply open my life to you
    and receive it.
Amen.

Day 7: Prepared for anything

Approach

Sovereign God,
    teach me that you are strong beyond words,
    faithful beyond comparison,
    and gracious beyond all comprehension –
    able to do more than I can ever ask or imagine,
    sufficient for all my needs.
Amen.

Read

God is our sanctuary and protection, a constant help in times of peril. So we will fear nothing, even if this world should be turned upside down and the mountains crumble into the depths of the ocean – even if the waters of the sea thunder and churn and the mountains quiver amidst the turmoil.
Psalm 46:1-3

Reflect

What will tomorrow bring? We have no way of knowing, do we? We may think we have everything planned, and life may indeed work out precisely as we envisage, but circumstances may equally conspire to bring about an altogether different chain of events. We can make an informed guess about what the future might hold, but we can never be sure, since life has a habit of springing surprises on us, for good or for ill. Any day, any moment, may unexpectedly bring joy or sorrow, pleasure or pain, health or sickness, life or death. So how do we face up to such uncertainty? We may, as Christians, feel secure about our eternal destiny, but how confident are we of coping with moments of tragedy and crisis; of facing whatever life might throw against us, and, however fierce the onslaught, standing firm? I have to say that in terms of my own ability to face such times I'm not confident at all. The thought of losing a loved one, struggling with illness, enduring pain or facing death fills me with dread. I simply have no idea how well or how badly I'd cope in such circumstances. Fortunately, however, it's not solely down to me just as it's not solely down to any of us in a similar situation. We have the assurance of God himself that his strength will be sufficient for all our needs, that nothing will ever be able to separate us from his love. If the Psalmist could write centuries ago, 'God is our sanctuary and protection, a constant help in times of peril. So we will fear nothing', how much more should we, with our experience and knowledge of Christ, be able to say the same? Not that we are in any way immune to suffering or disaster – there is no promise of that. What we do have, however, is God's promise to support us through such times. We may have no idea what the future holds or how we'll cope with it, but we can be confident that though *our* strength may fail, God's never will.

Pray

I shouldn't be scared Lord, I know that,
 but I can't help it sometimes.
When I look at the traumas some endure –
 the anguish of body, mind and spirit –
 I can't help wondering how I'd cope in their shoes,
 whether I'd hold on not simply to my faith
 but also to my sanity.
Should disaster strike, would I be brave,
 resilient in time of crisis?
I'd like to think so,
 but I doubt it somehow,
 a sense of panic welling up inside me even at the thought,
 never mind the real thing.
Lord, strengthen me.
Teach me that, whatever may come, you will be there;
 that, however fierce the storm, you will bring your peace.

Teach me to surrender my fear into your hands
and to entrust myself into your care,
secure in the assurance
that no matter what life or death may bring,
your purpose will continue
and your love remain sure.
In Christ's name I pray.
Amen.

Ponder

- Do you worry unnecessarily sometimes, brooding over what *might* be rather than coping with what *is*?
- Do you need to focus more on what God can do rather than on what *you* can't?
- In what ways have you found God to be a source of strength in the past? What words of Scripture speak most powerfully of the strength he has given to others?

Close

Sovereign God,
if sorrow, suffering, turmoil or trauma
should cause me to lose hold of you,
tighten your hold on me,
and, in your strength, see me safely through.
Amen.

Third week of Advent

A time to trust

The week ahead

A God we can depend on – that, in short, is the message tradition-ally emphasised during the third week of Advent. For centuries Christians have reminded themselves of the words of prophecy so wonderfully fulfilled in the coming of Christ: passages like Isaiah 9:2: 'The people who walked in darkness have seen a great light; those who lived in a land of deep darkness – on them light has shined'; like Isaiah 11:1: 'A shoot shall come out from the stock of Jesse, and a branch shall grow out of his roots'; like Micah 5:2a: 'But you, O Bethlehem of Ephrathath, who are one of the little clans of Judah, from you shall come forth for me one who is to rule in Israel'; like Malachi 3:2: 'But who can endure the day of his coming, and who can stand when he appears' (all passages from NRSV); and so we could go on. Each of these prophecies – originally addressed to and fulfilled in quite different situations – found infinitely greater fulfilment in the birth of Jesus and his subsequent life, death, resurrection and exaltation. In him, then, we see that God not only honours his promises but also goes on honouring them afresh to new generations. Though all else fails us, he will not; his faithfulness is assured. We will no doubt face troubles and tribulations like everyone else, as much tragedy, turmoil and testing as the next person, but we can still put our hand in his, confident that love will finally conquer hatred, good overcome evil, and life triumph over death. In that, let us put our trust.

Day 1: Trust in God's promises

Approach

Lord,
  remind me today of all you have done,
  and so may I trust more fully in all you will yet do.
Amen.

Read

I am God, and there is no other. I am God and there is none like me, pronouncing the end at the beginning and speaking at the dawn of time of things yet to be done, proclaiming, 'My will shall prevail, and I will fulfil my purpose.' I have spoken, and I will make it happen; I have planned, and I will accomplish it.
Isaiah 46:9-10, 11b

Reflect

'I promise to pay the bearer on demand the sum of five pounds.' That promise on a five-pound note, and similar assurances on notes of larger denominations, is as near to a cast-iron promise as we can get in this world. Barring complete financial meltdown, we can more or less guarantee that the note will be accepted anywhere in the country at its designated value, provided, of course, that it is not a forgery. Compare that with the sort of promise frequently made by politicians around election time: 'We will not raise taxes'; 'We will cut crime'; 'We will reduce waiting lists'; and so forth. Do we believe pledges like those? Somehow, I doubt it. We've seen too many made only to be broken. Cynicism is the order of the day.

What, then, of the promises of Scripture: how far can we trust them? Is it true that where two or three gather in the name of Christ, he will be there in the midst of them? Is it true that he will be with us always, to the end of time? Is it true that he will come again in glory? Is it true that whoever believes in him will not die but instead inherit eternal life? Is it true that nothing can ever separate us from the love of God, which is ours through Jesus Christ our Lord? The triumphant message of Advent is that not only these but all the promises God has given are true. Everything he has committed himself to do, he *will* do. Whatever he has said should happen, *will* happen. Trust him, come what may: we have his word.

Pray

Eternal God,
  I *say* I believe in your promises,
  but sometimes I'm not as sure as I'd like to be.
When it comes to stepping out in faith,
  taking risks for your kingdom;
  to receiving mercy,
  and accepting I'm truly forgiven;
  to death and resurrection,
  holding firm to the assurance you have given
  of life beyond the grave,
  I *do* believe,
  but my trust is fragile,
  threatened by doubts and questions,
  at risk of being broken.
Remind me of all you have already done across the years,
  the promises you have so wonderfully honoured
  and prophecies so gloriously fulfilled.
Remind me of the words I personally have found to be true
  and of the faithfulness
  that so many have experienced firsthand in turn.
So may I put my hand in yours
  and hold on to you more firmly,
  assured deep in my heart that your word is true,
  your love constant
  and your promises sure.

In Christ's name, I ask it.
Amen.

Ponder

- When did you last make time to reflect on God's promises? Which promises mean the most to you?
- Have disappointments in life caused you to lose sight of God's promises? Do you still have the same faith that he will honour them?
- What promises of God have you found realised in your own experience?

Close

Faithful God,
  teach me to step out in faith,
  trusting in your word,
  seeking your will
  and offering my commitment,
  and so I may recognise more fully the nearness of your presence,
  the truth of your promises,
  the constancy of your love
  and the wonder of your grace.
Amen.

Day 2: Trust in God's presence

Approach

Loving God,
    as I draw near to you now,
    teach me that you are with me always,
    and help me to sense your constant presence,
    through Jesus Christ my Lord.
Amen.

Read

I guarantee that I will be with you every day, to the very end of time.
Matthew 28:20

Reflect

One of the most popular of all Christian meditations must surely be the little poem 'Footprints in the Sand'. Its origins are contested – a 1964 version attributed to Margaret Fishback Powers but an earlier version, dated 1939, claimed for Mary Stevenson – yet what is beyond doubt is the phenomenal response to the poem, sales running into millions of copies and showing no signs of abating. This unprecedented success must surely indicate that the words speak directly to people's experience, helping to explain occasions when God has seemed strangely absent from their lives. We will all have experienced such times; moments of crisis and testing when we have cried out for help yet apparently waited in vain for an answer. We look for guidance, but none is forthcoming. We seek support, but feel we are on our own, left to fend for ourselves as best we can. At times like those, faith can teeter on the brink. Is God truly there, we can't help asking, or have we been deluding ourselves? The answer given in 'Footprints', as in Scripture generally, is not only that God is with us all along, even when we do not see him, but that he is especially near in times of crisis, carrying us on his shoulders and seeing us safely through.

That truth lies at the heart of Advent, for this is a season not just about the past or future but, above all, about the present, life here and now. We celebrate the coming of Christ, Emmanuel: God with us – and that title means just what it says: that though it may not be apparent, and though it may sometimes seem anything but the case, God *is* with us, every moment, every hour of every day, now and always. Thanks be to God!

Pray

I shouldn't have doubted, Lord, I know that,
    but I couldn't help it,
    for I called and you didn't seem to answer,
    I searched but never seemed to find,
    and all of a sudden you felt distant,
    detached,
    disinterested,
    no longer part of my daily life,
    no longer part of anything.
I kept faith as best I could, believe me,
    but each day it was that little bit harder,
    conviction starting to crumble and questions to grow
    as still you appeared absent –
    aloof to my plight,
    remote from this world.
But then, piece by piece, the jigsaw came together,
    hindsight revealing what was hidden at the time:
    that you'd been there all along –
    holding,
    guiding,
    loving,
    caring,
    supporting me when I stumbled,

carrying me when I fell –
always close by my side.
Thank you, Lord, that whether I see it or whether I don't,
your hand is upon me;
that however remote you may seem,
you are always near –
unrecognised perhaps,
unnoticed,
but unfailing.
In that knowledge, I will put my trust,
this and every day.
Amen.

Ponder

- At what times have you been most conscious of God's presence?
- In what ways do you sense God's nearness? What might cause you to lose sight of it?
- Can you recall occasions when God has seemed absent but in which, with the benefit of hindsight, you can see he was at work?

Close

Gracious God,
go with me in my journey of life,
and though I do not always recognise your presence
or appreciate your nearness,
walk close by my side,
leading, supporting, encouraging and providing,
until I have finished my course
and see you face to face,
through Jesus Christ my Lord.
Amen.

Day 3: Trust in God's patience

Approach

Merciful God,
  though I have been weak in your service
  and faithless in discipleship,
  reach out still in your grace.
Touch this moment with your truth,
  and each day with your love,
  through Jesus Christ my Lord.
Amen.

Read

You are forgiving, O Lord, a merciful God, dependable, slow to anger, and overflowing in patience.
Psalm 86:15

Reflect

'How many more times must I tell you not to do that!' When's the last time you uttered words such as those? Unless I'm much mistaken, it won't have been so long ago. No matter how patient we are, there comes a point when we've had enough; when, unable to restrain ourselves any longer, we explode in anger or frustration. We don't mind putting up with the occasional irritation, the odd mistake, but when someone goes on committing the same error *ad infinitum* something inside finally snaps. If that's true in trivial matters, it's all the more so in important issues. Anyone who has been betrayed in a relationship, cheated in a financial transaction, let down in a promise, or subjected to cruelty, will find it very hard truly to forgive, let alone to trust again the one who failed or hurt them. We might perhaps give another chance in exceptional circumstances – possibly even several chances – but eventually the patience of even the most saintly will be tested to breaking point.

Understandably, we tend to assume that God reacts in the same way. For all our talk of his limitless grace and unbounded love, we find it hard to imagine that he can feel any differently than we do, and, in consequence, the more we fail him, the more burdened we become by a sense of guilt. 'Can he still forgive me?' we ask. 'After all the mistakes I've made, all the times I've asked forgiveness for the same old weaknesses, the same sins, can he truly be ready to wipe the slate clean yet again?' It seems incredible, too much to hope for, and so, though we dutifully offer our prayers of confession, we have no real sense of being forgiven, of the weight of guilt being lifted.

If that's how you feel, stop and think again, for your picture of God couldn't be more wrong. As Psalm 85 reminds us, he is slow to anger and overflowing in patience, always ready to forgive and forget. If you doubt that, remember how Peter approached Jesus with a question similar to the one we've been asking: 'Lord, how often should I let someone sin against me and still forgive them – as many as seven times?' 'Not seven times,' says Jesus, 'but seventy-seven times' (Matthew 18:21-22). In other words, forgive as many times as you're asked to. Why? Because that's how God forgives us, his patience never exhausted, his grace never spent. You may make the same mistakes today you've made every day for the last twenty years. You may exhibit the same flaws, fall prey to the same temptations, display the same faults – it makes no difference, God is still ready to pardon. Yes, our failure will grieve him, and yes, he will hope for better things, but so long as we are truly sorry, then his nature is always to show mercy. Don't struggle through life with a sense of unresolved guilt, a burden of shame; bring your mistakes once more to God and trust in his patience.

Pray

'Oh no! Not again!'
I don't know about you, Lord,
   but that's what I felt like saying:
   a howl of despair,
   groan of frustration,
   as once more I made the same mistake,
   displaying the same weakness,
   the same flaw,
   as so many times before.
Could you still have patience,
   still forgive?
I know I couldn't.
I'd have long since lashed out in fury or simply walked away,
   such persistent folly and feeble resolve too much to bear.
Yet not you, Lord.
Somehow,
   despite it all,
   you reach out, time and again, with the same welcome,
   the same warmth,
   ready yet again to let bygones be bygones,
   to put the past behind me and let me start afresh.
I don't understand such forbearance,
   such grace,
   such love,
   but I praise you for it,
   for in you alone I find one ready to see the worst
   and yet believe the best;
   to see what I am
   and still keep faith in what I might become.
Lord, for bearing with me,
   for your awesome, amazing patience,
   receive my heartfelt undying thanks,
   in the name of Christ.
Amen.

79

Ponder

- Are there aspects of your life that you believe God will find hard to forgive? Is this because you are not genuinely sorry about these, or because you fear God may lose patience with you?
- Do you still wrestle with feelings of guilt over your weaknesses and mistakes? Have you understood the message of God's forgiveness in Christ?
- How far is the patience God shows to you reflected in your dealings with others?

Close

Gracious God,
show me where my discipleship is weak,
my commitment flawed
and my life found wanting,
and, by your grace, help me
to become more like the person you would have me be,
through Jesus Christ my Lord.
Amen.

Day 4: Trust in God's justice

Approach

Almighty God,
    teach me each day to know and love you better,
    so that all I am and do
    may be pleasing in your sight.
Amen.

Read

Lord God, bringer of retribution, God of reckoning, shine among us! Arise, you arbiter of this world, and put the smug and self-opinionated in their place! How long, Lord, shall the wicked prosper, how long will they gloat? The Lord will not abandon his people or go back on the birthright he has promised. The faithful and all who pursue what is good will, in time, receive justice.
Psalm 94:1-3, 14-15

Reflect

'How long, Lord, shall the wicked prosper?' So asks the writer of Psalm 94, and it's a good question, one that many of us will frequently have echoed during the course of our life. We like to think that we live in a moral universe, in a world where virtue is rewarded and wrongdoing is punished, where good ultimately triumphs over evil, but the more we experience, the harder it is sometimes to continue believing in such things. All too often the innocent suffer and the good are taken for a ride, while greed, corruption and exploitation not only go unchecked but also prove lucrative into the bargain. Why go by the book, we can't help but ask, when others throw it out of the window? Why play straight when others are happy to toss caution to the wind? Is there truly any justice in this world, any calling to account, or are all such ideas simply naïve illusion?

Advent is a season that emphatically affirms the former, antici-pating a time when each of us will have to answer for our actions, a day of reckoning when judgement will finally be passed. But if that lies in the future, there is surely also an element of judgement here and now, in that whatever rewards evil may bring, it is pow-erless ultimately to satisfy, incapable of offering true contentment and as often as not bringing its own heavy price. We cannot prove that assertion, and indeed some will dispute it, but the fulfilment we seek, the blessings we experience and the joys we celebrate as Christians are of a kind that this world cannot offer. What others might count poor are to us riches beyond comparison.

It can sometimes be hard, faced by the injustices of life, not to question and wonder about the justice of God, but don't get drawn along that road, for it is to mistake pleasure on earth for treasure in heaven. However things may seem, Advent calls us to trust in God's justice, which one day will become clear.

Pray

Lord,
    try as I might I can't help questioning sometimes,
    can't help wondering why evil seems to prosper
    and good go unrewarded.
I know that shouldn't matter –
    that there's more to life than money,
    power,
    prestige,
    possessions –
    but occasionally it gets to me nonetheless,
    so that I doubt not only your justice
    but also whether you're even there at all.
How can you ignore wrongdoing,
    overlook so much that flouts your will,
    not just turning a blind eye
    but allowing evil to flourish while virtue goes to the wall?
It doesn't make sense –

82

life sometimes an enigma
and faith a puzzle.
Only that, of course, is seeing things my way,
according to my values,
my yardstick,
confusing worldly wealth with divine blessing,
earthly pleasure with eternal fulfilment.
Forgive me, Lord,
and teach me to trust in your justice,
recognising that you alone can see into the heart
and weigh our lives in the balance.
Teach me, then, to look to myself,
and to leave the verdict on others to you.
In Christ's name I pray.
Amen.

Ponder

- What injustices in this world do you find hardest to reconcile with your faith?
- Is it true that crime doesn't pay? If so, can this idea be extended to help resolve issues of injustice?
- How far do you think God's justice is limited to the life to come?

Close

Mighty and mysterious God,
I cannot answer for others
but I will have to answer for myself.
Teach me, then, to serve you faithfully,
to love you truly, in word and deed,
and to trust finally in your redeeming grace
on which we all depend,
through Jesus Christ our Lord.
Amen.

Day 5: Trust in God's peace

Approach

Loving God,
    as I draw near to you,
    draw near to me.
Encircling me in your love,
    enable me by your power,
    enthuse me by your grace,
    enfold me in your peace,
    in Jesus' name.
Amen.

Read

Glory to God in the highest heaven, and peace on earth among all on whom his favour rests!
Luke 2:14

Reflect

What do we mean by the word 'peace'? The reality, of course, is that we can mean very different things. To a hippie in the 1960s the word was a form of greeting, summing up an attitude of live and let live. For others, it speaks primarily of harmony and an end to war, as witnessed by the proliferation of peace camps, vigils, protestors and marches, not to mention peace agreements, accords and processes. For others again, the word conjures up images of tranquillity: a quiet place, perhaps, away from it all; while for yet others it represents an inner calmness – what we might call 'peace of mind' or 'being at peace' – freed from the stresses and tensions of daily life. All these highlight valid aspects of peace, yet none captures the whole.

An understanding closer to achieving this is the Jewish idea of *shalom*. On one level, this is simply another form of greeting, not so far removed from the hippie 'Peace', but, properly understood, it is much more, denoting wholeness and health, joy and fulfilment, serenity of spirit and general contentment – a sense of being at concord with oneself, the world and God. To enjoy *shalom*, then, would indeed be a blessing, though most Jews when they use this word, probably have in mind an ideal state rather than an experienced reality, something wished for rather than expected.

There is, though, one other understanding of peace we have not yet explored: namely the peace of God promised by Jesus to his followers. 'Peace is my bequest to you – my own peace; unlike anything the world can give. So, then, do not be anxious or fearful in heart' (John 14:27). What is this peace? By definition we cannot fully describe it, since it is not of this world, but we can at least point to some of its key aspects. It is the peace arising from an assurance of God's love in all circumstances, from enjoying liberation from bondage to sin and guilt, from experiencing the daily reality of God's presence, and from knowing that our ultimate destiny is guaranteed – each of these and far more reinforced by the presence of God's Spirit deep within; a peace, in other words, that comes through discovering the ground of our being, meaning to our existence, an end to our inner restlessness and striving. Here is the peace that has somehow sustained people in the midst of the most appalling suffering and severest testing; the peace spoken of by the Apostle Paul that passes all understanding. Words cannot suffice to express this most precious of gifts, but words are not needed. It is open to all, offered freely, lovingly and constantly in Christ, the King of kings and Lord of lords – the Prince of Peace.

Pray

I looked for peace, Lord,
  but I didn't find it.
I looked at the world,
  but I saw there division and discord –
  person divided against person
  and nation against nation;
  hatred, greed and bitterness
  exploding into violence and war.

I looked at myself,
    but I saw there a restless striving for contentment,
    an outward calm masking an inner turmoil.
I looked at the Church,
    and even there the wounds ran deep,
    conflict over worship and doctrine,
    clashes of temperament and personality,
    petty disputes dividing Christian from Christian,
    fellowship from fellowship,
    estranging us from you and one another.
I looked for peace, Lord,
    and I didn't find it,
    until I looked to you,
    and then I found rest for my soul,
    a haven from the storm,
    a quietness deep within.
Lord,
    for that precious gift,
    receive my praise.
Amen.

Ponder

- How broad a sense do you have of God's peace? Do you tend to over-emphasise one aspect – peace of mind, world peace, for example – at the cost of others?
- Do you face up to those things in your life that deny peace, whether in terms of relationships or of personal peace?
- How would you describe the peace that God gives?

Close

Gracious God,
    when the storm rages and life is in turmoil,
    when the wind blows and the waves threaten to engulf me,
    grant that even then my soul will be at peace,
    secure in the constancy of your love.
Amen.

Day 6: Trust in God's transforming grace

Approach

Living God,
   I come to you as I am.
Meet me through your word,
   through your Spirit,
   through the living presence of the risen Christ,
   and so direct what I shall be,
   to the glory of your name.
Amen.

Read

Anyone united with Christ is a new creation; the old self has passed away in its entirety; everything is made new.
2 Corinthians 5:17

Reflect

It's one thing to recognise that all is not as it should be, quite another to put things right. That is as true in terms of discipleship as anything. Most of us will be ready enough to admit our weaknesses but when it comes to changing for the better we wring our hands in despair. We might have nurtured such hopes once, the early days of commitment marked by the conviction that, with God's help, we would conquer our failings, eradicate our faults, but as the years pass and many of those flaws stubbornly persist it becomes increasingly harder to maintain such idealism. Our attitude instead echoes the famous outpouring of frustration by the Apostle Paul at his inability to live the sort of life he wants to, doing instead those things he has no desire to do. Yet if that is one side of the Apostle Paul, there is another, summed up in the words of our reading. In Christ, he says, we are a new creation, the old being done away with, put behind us. What does he mean? How can we square those words with the daily experience of failure that Paul himself speaks of? The answer is that Paul refers here to how God perceives us rather than how we actually are. We are accepted by grace, reckoned as guiltless through what Christ has done for us on the cross. Yet this does not mean that the change is purely cosmetic. On the contrary, God is constantly at work within us, transforming, redeeming and renewing. We cannot change by ourselves, as anyone who has tried making New Year or Lenten resolutions will know all too well, but what *we* cannot do, *he* can.

Pray

I can't change, Lord!
I'd *like* to,
    and I *try* to,
    but you can see for yourself,
    after all these years,
    that it's no good,
    my every attempt doomed to failure,
    my intentions good but the results feeble.
I've done my best, heaven knows,
    striving every day to follow more faithfully,
    but all my efforts have come to nothing,
    the spirit willing but the flesh weak.
Yet, what am I saying?
I'm wrong again,
    for it's not down to me –
    my resolve,
    my will –
    but to your grace,
    your redeeming, renewing touch;
    you alone able to change the inside,

to effect a new creation,
to take what is and shape what will be.
Forgive me, Lord, for yet again turning faith into works,
    confusing what is impossible for me
    with what is possible with you.
Forgive me for losing sight
    of your transforming power and restoring love.
Draw me closer to you, so that you may work within me,
    taking what I am and, by your grace,
    fashioning what I may yet become,
    to the glory of your name.
Amen.

Ponder

- Have you allowed repeated failure to close your mind to the possibility of real change in your life? Have you lost sight of the way God can still work within you?

- Are there people or situations you have come to despair of, believing them to be beyond redemption? Again, do you need to reappraise things in terms of what God is able to do?

- Are you guilty sometimes of striving to change yourself, rather than nurturing your relationship with God and letting his transforming power change you from within?

Close

Sovereign God,
    when I resist the prospect of change, challenge me;
    when I see no need for change, forgive me;
    when I lose hope in the possibility of change, inspire me.
Help me to open my life to what you want to do,
    what you need to do
    and what you *shall* do,
    through the grace and power of Christ my Lord.
Amen.

Day 7: Trust in God's renewing power

Approach

Sovereign God,
  meet with me now
  so that I may give you not just these few moments set aside
  but my all –
  my worship,
  my service,
  my love,
  my life.
Take me and use me in the work of your kingdom,
  to your glory.
Amen.

Read

Behold, I make all things new.
Revelation 21:5

Reflect

It's often remarked that we grow more set in our opinions and more conservative in our attitudes as the years go by. Many who in their teenage years are angry young liberals end up as pillars of the establishment, staunchly defending in later life what they had once so vigorously challenged. The celebrated poet William Wordsworth, for example, was considered such a radical as a young man that he was suspected of subversive activity, but he was to become a bastion of orthodoxy in later life.

We may not change our ideals quite so sharply, but most of us find it hard to maintain the level of idealism that marked our youth. As we see yet another famine, yet further conflict, yet more injustice, we become hardened by it, no longer seriously expecting the world to change. Can there be an end to hatred and violence, injustice and exploitation? It seems impossible. Might the world one day be freed from the blight of hunger, poverty, greed and bitterness? Who are we kidding? Quite simply, we've seen such things so many times before that we lose faith they can be any different.

So does it make sense to talk as Christians of good defeating evil, hope conquering despair, and love triumphing over hatred? Can we meaningfully talk of God's kingdom beginning here on earth? If such matters were dependent solely upon us, the answer would have to be no. We cannot even change ourselves, let alone the world. But the change that the gospel speaks of rests not with us but with God, a God who in Christ changed the course of history, transforming innumerable lives across the years; who, taking human flesh, brought light into the world, which darkness, for all its efforts, has been unable to overcome. At the heart of our faith is the conviction that God is able to make not just us but all things new (Revelation 21:5). This is, of course, an ongoing process, which, like so much, will not be completed until the fulfilment of his kingdom, but it starts now, for God is able to transform every situation, no matter how hopeless it may seem. No person is beyond his saving touch, no circumstances too hopeless to be turned around. It may not feel like it sometimes – indeed, we may once again feel that nothing can ever change – but what seems impossible to us is possible with God. Advent calls us never to lose faith in what he is able to do, never to lose heart, but instead to trust in the new beginnings he is constantly seeking to bring.

Pray

Lord God,
I used to believe this world could be different –
that love could overcome hate,
good conquer evil
and joy triumph over sorrow –
but I'm not so sure now.

I do still believe it –
    or, at least, part of me does –
    but not with the same passion and intensity I once felt,
    faith being tinged with doubt,
    hope coloured by despair.
There have been too many disappointments,
    too many false dawns,
    each promising so much
    yet delivering so little.
One tyranny ends,
    another begins.
One wrong is righted,
    another takes its place.
The faces may be different
    but human nature stays depressingly the same,
    and it's hard,
    so very hard,
    to keep faith alive –
    to accept that anything can really change.
Lord,
    remind me of all you did in Christ . . .
    and all you continue to do through him.
Speak to me of the lives you have transformed,
    and of those you are still transforming.
Help me to glimpse again the wholeness you have brought,
    the commitment you've inspired
    and the service offered in your name;
    each a symbol of your renewing, redeeming love.
Break through the walls of disillusionment and despondency,
    and revive a sense of all you are able to do,
    all you *will* do,
    and all you are doing *even now*,
    through Jesus Christ,
    the King of kings and Lord of lords.
Amen.

Ponder

- Have you allowed yourself to dwell on the bad rather than the good in life, on human evil rather than God's goodness?
- Have you lost sight of the way God has worked in so many lives, including your own?
- In what situations and people have you seen God's renewing power at work?

Close

Teach me, Lord, wherever I lose hope
    to remember that what is impossible for me is possible for you;
    that what *I* can't change, *you* can.
Teach me, then, to keep faith in your purpose,
    whatever appearances might seem to say,
    and to give my all for the growth of your kingdom,
    to the glory of your name.
Amen.

Fourth week of Advent

A time to respond

The week ahead

'Let it be to me just as you say.' Those words of Mary have been celebrated across the years as the paradigm of Christian commitment, a classic example of the sort of response God yearns to see from us all. But, of course, it was not the only response to the coming of Christ, just as it is not the only response today. Many then, as now, responded wholeheartedly enough, others were lukewarm or undecided, while others still were hostile, their attitude one of rejection rather than welcome. This week, then, we focus on some of those responses, starting with that unforgettable reply of Mary's, asking each time not only how they reacted but how we respond today.

Day 1: An unreserved response

Approach

Living God,
   remind me of what you are able to achieve
   rather than what I might accomplish in my own power.
Teach me, then, to seek your will,
   and to respond in faith,
   through Christ my Lord.
Amen.

Read

Now in the sixth month the angel Gabriel was sent by God to a town in Galilee called Nazareth, to a virgin engaged to a man named Joseph, a member of the house of David. The virgin's name was Mary. Approaching her, he said, 'Greetings, you who have been highly favoured. The Lord is with you.' She was bewildered by his words, and contemplated what such a greeting might mean. The angel said to her, 'Don't be frightened, Mary, for you have found favour with God. You will conceive in your womb and bear a son, and you will give him the name "Jesus". He will be great, and will be called the Son of the Most High, and the Lord God will give him the throne of his ancestor David. He will reign over the house of Jacob for ever, and his kingdom will never end.' Mary said to the angel, 'How can this be, since I am a virgin?' The angel answered, 'The Holy Spirit will come upon you, and the power of the Most High will rest over you, so that the child you will bear will be called the Son of God, for with God nothing is impossible.' Mary responded, 'I am the Lord's servant. Let it be to me just as you say.'
Luke 1:26-35, 38

Reflect

Reading again the words of Mary in response to Gabriel, I was struck, as never before, by the parallel with the words of Jesus in Gethsemane: 'Not my will, but yours be done.' That, effectively, is what Mary said here to God. The challenge he had brought was an onerous one: not so much to bear a child – though, as any parent will know, that is demanding if also hugely enriching – but to bear also opprobrium as a mother whose child was born out of wedlock, as well as the responsibility of conceiving and nurturing God's Son, with all the possibilities and demands attendant upon that. It must have been tempting to prevaricate, desperately hard not to quibble. Couldn't she be given time to think things over? Could God give her a clearer picture of what the future might hold, of what he was actually asking, and of what guarantees he could give she would measure up to the task? A host of questions must have welled up in her mind besides the obvious riposte, 'How can this be, since I am a virgin?' But the answer given to that single question answered everything, for it approached the situation not from her perspective, but from God's, for whom nothing is impossible. That, apparently, for Mary was enough. 'Let it be to me just as you say', or, to put it another way, 'Not my will, but yours be done.'

Do we have that same confidence in the power of God? Do we have a similar willingness to trust in his purpose? Are we ready to respond to his call, to do whatever he asks of us? Mary, like anyone else, had questions for which she sought answers, but she was ready nonetheless to give an unreserved 'yes' to God's desire to use her. Are we ready to do the same?

Pray

Lord,
  I thought I'd responded,
  that I'd professed my faith and offered my commitment,
  but I hadn't,
  not fully,
  not as you wanted me to.

I'd offered a part of me,
but the rest was still firmly mine,
ring-fenced,
not to be disturbed,
kept quietly away from any challenge you might bring.
I was ready to serve,
so long as your goals were mine,
ready to follow,
so long as our paths coincided,
but the thought of loving proving costly,
discipleship bringing demands,
well, quite simply I pushed it aside,
hoping that what I couldn't see I could safely ignore.
Only I couldn't,
for instead of having a foot in both camps,
I didn't have one in either,
life lived neither fully for me or fully for you.
Forgive me, Lord,
and teach me to consecrate myself wholly to your service:
to be used as you would use me,
to serve as you would have me serve,
confident that though I may not have the resources needed,
your strength will see me through.
In the name of Christ, I ask it.
Amen.

Ponder

- What things hold you back from committing yourself fully to God's service?

- Are there areas of your life that faith doesn't touch? Does your worship each Sunday spill over into the way you live your life every day?

- Are you resisting something that God is calling you to do? Why? Is it time you responded in faith?

Close

Loving God,
    show me where you can use me,
    remind me how you have blessed me,
    teach me how much you love me,
    and so help me to respond as freely and wholeheartedly to you
    as you have responded to me in Christ.
Amen.

Day 2: A humble response

Approach

Mighty God,
 teach me what I can do for you
 and give me grace to do it,
 to your glory.
Amen.

Read

This is what happened concerning the birth of Jesus Christ. While his mother, Mary, was engaged to Joseph, but before they lived together, the Holy Spirit caused her to become pregnant. Being a man of principle, Joseph was reluctant to see her disgraced publicly, so he made plans to end the engagement quietly. Just when he'd made this decision, however, an angel of the Lord appeared to him in a dream, saying, 'Joseph, son of David, have no qualms about marrying Mary, for the child she carries originates from the Holy Spirit. She will bear a son, and you are to call him Jesus, for he will save his people from their sins.' This all took place to fulfil what the Lord had said through the prophet: 'Look, the virgin will conceive and bear a son, and they will call him "Emmanuel", meaning, "God is with us".' When he awoke, Joseph did as the angel of the Lord had instructed, taking Mary as his wife, but he did not make love to her until she gave birth to a son; and he named him Jesus.
Matthew 1:18-25

Reflect

Nobody likes being made a fool of, do they? To be exposed to public ridicule, held up as a laughing stock, is a deeply humiliating experience and one that we'd go to considerable lengths to avoid.

I'm sure Joseph was no exception; indeed, there's no doubt about it, as his initial reaction to the news of Mary's pregnancy makes clear. He was, of course, engaged to marry her, and in Jewish society that represented a formally binding contract akin to marriage itself. Furthermore, according to Jewish law, this meant that Mary was subject to his authority; almost, we might say, his possession. The discovery, then, that she was expecting a child must not only have come as an enormous shock but would also have brought with it the potential stigma of having been cuckolded by his betrothed, what was rightly his having been appropriated by another. No wonder Joseph toyed with the idea of quietly breaking off the engagement – anything that might hush up a scandal was worth trying. Then, though, came his dream and the call not to put Mary aside but to marry her, the child she carried conceived not by another man but by God. That must have taken some believing, however vivid his dream, and it must equally have taken some courage to proceed with the wedding, knowing how tongues would wag as the pregnancy advanced and people began to count the days between the wedding and the birth. Above all, though, the course he followed must have taken enormous humility, more even perhaps than that shown by Mary. She, at least, had the honour of bearing God's Son and, in a special way, of him being part of her, conceived in and delivered from her womb. Joseph had none of that, just the sly grins and knowing looks to put up with. His was very much a supporting role: to be there for Mary and Jesus, providing for their needs, offering a secure home environment, fulfilling a father's role even though he was not in any biological sense the father. Yet he willingly put God first and himself last, more concerned with God's will and with the needs of his wife and her child than his own interests.

Are we willing to put God first – to do what he asks of us without any thought of reward? Are we ready to endure misunderstanding and perhaps scorn for his sake, to be considered fools for Christ if that's what our calling demands? Are we prepared, if necessary, to be one of the supporting cast in God's purposes, taking a minor role, a bit part, enabling others to occupy centre-stage and fulfil their God-given task? That's what Joseph did, his role so different to that of Mary. While many continue to honour her as an example of faith and obedience, he, by comparison, scarcely gets a mention, but his contribution was no less real or valuable.

Pray

I don't mind taking a back seat, Lord,
   I really don't,
   for I'm not one to hog the limelight,
   thrust myself forward.
I'm happy with a bit part in the supporting cast,
   never comfortable on centre-stage.
But a spot of recognition wouldn't come amiss;
   nothing fancy,
   just the occasional word of appreciation
   or gesture of thanks –
   enough to let me know that someone, somewhere,
   understands what I do
   and why I do it.
Yet, small though that seems,
   it's too much, isn't it,
   for it's still about me rather than you,
   my ego rather than *your* glory.
Forgive me, Lord,
   and teach me to be ready to serve you
   with no thought of reward
   and no concern for self,
   ready to be mocked,
   mistaken,
   misunderstood for your sake.
Use me as you will,
   no matter how humble my role might be,
   so that I might further your kingdom
   and contribute to your purpose.
Amen.

Ponder

- How ready are you to undertake work for which there is little or no recognition?
- Do you put limits on the way God can use you? Do you expect him to fit in with your expectations or are you willing to fit in with his?
- Are you willing to put up with misunderstanding and even mockery for the sake of the gospel?

Close

Gracious God,
    teach me to seek not my glory but yours,
    not my will but your purpose,
    not my well-being but your kingdom.
Use me as you see fit,
    in your service.
Amen.

Day 3: An indifferent response

Approach

Merciful God,
    stir my imagination at the magnitude of your love,
    kindle my heart at the immensity of your grace,
    and so may I respond afresh each day to the good news of Christ,
    serving him faithfully in body, mind and spirit.,
    to your praise and glory.
Amen.

Read

He entered the world – a world that owed its very existence to him; yet the world did not recognise him. He came to those who were his own, but his own people did not acknowledge him.
John 1:10-11

Reflect

One of the great scandals of history is that words like those above from John's Gospel have been used to foster anti-Semitism; to justify hatred and persecution of Jews on the pretext that they as a nation crucified Christ. Few things could have been further from John's mind or from the testimony of Scripture as a whole. Admittedly, John used the expression 'the Jews' in a pejorative sense, but he had in mind when doing so not the Jewish race as such but those within it who rejected Jesus; generally speaking, the Sadducees, scribes and Pharisees – the religious establishment of his day. To understand the import of John's words for the past, present and future, we need to cast the net wider, for the challenge he brings concerns all. As fellow human beings, we are all 'his own people', those for whom Christ came into the world and to whom he continues to come through his Holy Spirit. Are we ready to receive him? Do we truly make room for him in our lives, giving him not just any old place but *pride* of place? Thankfully, few today are opposed to Christianity (although, as we shall see in our next session, we may encounter hostility on occasions). The problem today is rather that the gospel, at least outside the Church, rarely stirs up strong feelings either way. The most common reaction – and perhaps the greatest threat – is apathy, a total indifference to whatever the gospel has to say. In part this reflects the Church's failure to move with the times; an inability to adapt its worship, structures and activities in a way that remains faithful to its roots yet speaks relevantly to modern-day issues. In part it reflects a failure among Christians to wrestle with questions of faith, retreating instead into a naïve fundamentalism that serves only to estrange the majority of thinking people. Perhaps, though, in largest part, it reflects a desire to sidestep the disturbing challenge of Christ, a reluctance to contemplate what might unsettle people's comfortable lifestyles. Rather than admit to the possibility of awkward home truths, many prefer simply to look the other way.

Is that true of us? We may count ourselves Christians, we may nominally attend church, we may offer up the occasional prayer, we may even be active church members, yet still be largely indifferent to the claims of Christ upon our life. Before we shake our heads at the indifference of others, let us ask a few honest questions of ourselves. Does the reality of Christ's presence shape the way we live? Does what we believe show itself in the people we are?

Pray

Lord,
   I stopped today,
   shocked and shaken,
   for I realised I'd barely thought of you for days,
   weeks,
   even months.
I'd gone through the motions –
   attending church,

offering the occasional prayer –
but effectively I'd gone my own way,
without reference to you,
without seeking your will,
faith simply not an issue in the daily round of life.
I'd not rebelled,
nothing like that –
not set out to be disobedient,
to resist your will
or to ignore your presence –
but in a way I wish I had,
for it's worse, my mistake:
not hostility but indifference,
a sorry case of disinterest rather than rejection.
Forgive me, Lord,
for little by little I've lost touch,
neglecting my side of our relationship,
casual in discipleship;
and slowly love has grown cold,
commitment weak,
faith fractured.
Confront me again with your living word,
challenge me through the grace of Christ,
stir me by your mighty Spirit,
and so kindle the flame of trust and the fire of love within me;
a response from the heart made new each day.
Amen.

Ponder

- Do you make enough room in your life for Christ? Do you give him a central place or fit him in somewhere on the periphery?
- Are there areas of your life that faith doesn't touch?
- How would you attempt to counter the indifference of others to the message of the gospel? How would you sum up its challenge for today?

Close

Gracious God,
    when faith grows cold, rekindle it;
    when commitment grows weak, strengthen it;
    when love fades, restore it;
    when vision withers, revive it.
Break afresh into my life and breathe your Spirit upon me,
    so that I may know and respond to you with all my heart,
    and live each day to your glory,
    through Jesus Christ my Lord.
Amen.

Day 4: A hostile response

Approach

Mighty God,
    so meet with me and work within my heart
    that my faith may show itself in action
    and my life present the challenge of the gospel.
Amen.

Read

When Herod realised that the wise men had fooled him, he was livid. Working out the timescale from what the wise men had told him, he gave orders that all children aged two or under living in or near Bethlehem should be executed. So the prophecy of Jeremiah was fulfilled: 'A voice was heard in Ramah, loud howls and expressions of grief, Rachel sobbing for her offspring; inconsolable because they had been slaughtered.'
Matthew 2:16-18

Reflect

Living as we do in a nominally Christian country, we can forget sometimes that discipleship for some across the centuries has involved hostility and persecution. It was true, of course, in the days of the early Church, as testified to in the letter to the Hebrews with its graphic and horrifying accounts of the barbaric treatment meted out by the authorities. Indeed, for countless years, until the adoption of Christianity as the official religion of Rome, innumerable Christians were routinely tortured, maimed and killed for their faith. More recently, Christians have suffered repression in countries in the Eastern bloc up until the lifting of the Iron Curtain, and even today there are countries where Christianity is at best tolerated and frequently the target of hatred and violence.

How would we fare in such circumstances? How many of us would hold on to our faith, still less make a public stand for it, if it put our safety at risk? I very much doubt I'd have the courage to do so. Thankfully, we are unlikely to be put to the test, but that doesn't mean we will experience no hostility at all. None of us, of course, would go looking for it, any more than a Christian in ancient Rome or Eastern Europe would have courted trouble, but there are times when, if we are to be true to Christ, we must make a stand for what we believe in, even though that might prove unpopular. It may mean speaking up on a point of principle when others stay silent; it may mean pricking people's conscience when they prefer to ignore evil; it may mean challenging wrongdoing when others turn a blind eye – in each case not in a narrow judgemental way, setting ourselves above others, but simply holding out for what we believe to be right. Would we, if necessary, have the faith and courage to risk opposition for the sake of Christ? Few of us, I'm sure, would relish a hostile response, but there might just come situations when even that is better than no response at all.

Pray

Lord,
    I don't like trouble;
    in fact it terrifies me,
    the very thought sending shivers down my spine,
    so I steer well clear,
    avoiding controversy,
    keeping my head down,
    restricting my faith, as far as possible,
    to something between me and you,
    no one else.
Yet, in my heart, I know that will not do,
    for there have been times –
    far too many –
    when I should have stood firm,
    stuck my neck out,

and failed to do so.
I saw injustice,
   and kept quiet;
   witnessed evil,
   and looked the other way;
   each time claiming it wasn't my business,
   not my job to get involved.
But it was,
   for if *I* ignore it *others* will do the same,
   and what's done to one today will be done to many tomorrow,
   perhaps even to me.
Teach me, Lord, when necessary, to risk conflict,
   even hostility,
   for the sake of truth;
   to endure resentment,
   unpopularity,
   for the sake of right;
   to face hardship, even danger,
   for the sake of good.
Teach me to stand up for the values of your kingdom,
   ready to risk some cost for you who paid the ultimate price
   in Jesus Christ my Lord.
Amen.

Ponder

- Has staying true to Christ ever made you unpopular, or provoked hostility?

- Have there been times when you kept silent when you should have spoken out, or when you turned a blind eye to what you knew to be wrong rather than risk antagonism? Why was this?

- Is there a stand you need to make now, despite what it might cost you?

Close

Sovereign God,
  when discipleship involves confronting evil
  and commitment means standing up to be counted,
  grant me courage to stay true to you
  and to accept the cost,
  through Jesus Christ my Lord.
Amen.

Day 5: A personal response

Approach

Loving God,
    as you have opened your heart to me,
    so help me now and always to open my heart to you,
    in joyful response
    and grateful service.
Amen.

Read

There were shepherds in that area, living in the fields and keeping watch over their flock during the night. Suddenly, an angel of the Lord appeared to them, and the glory of the Lord shone around them, and they were overcome with terror. However, the angel said to them, 'There's nothing to be frightened of; for see – I am bringing you good news of great joy that is for all people: today a Saviour has been born to you in the city of David, who is Christ the Lord. Let this be a sign to you: you will find a child swaddled in strips of cloth and lying in a manger.' All at once there was with the angel rank on rank of other heavenly beings, praising God and saying, 'Glory to God in the highest heaven, and peace on earth among all on whom his favour rests!' When the angels had departed and returned to heaven, the shepherds said to each other, 'Let us go, then, to Bethlehem and see this event that has taken place, which the Lord has made known to us.' So they came with haste, and found Mary and Joseph, and the baby lying in a manger.
Luke 2:8-16

Reflect

Do you remember the total eclipse of the sun a few years back? The chances are that you won't, for when the long-awaited moment came, much of the UK was shrouded in cloud if not a steady stream of drizzle. Yet, despite the vagaries of the British climate and the knowledge that rain was forecast, countless people had assembled across the country – especially where I live in the West Country – to witness the spectacle, hoping to catch at least a glimpse of this spectacular solar event. The interest was wholly understandable: for many it was a once-in-a-lifetime opportunity and they didn't want to miss it. Yes, there would be televised pictures from vantage points across the world, each showing the eclipse in infinitely more detail, but there's nothing to touch seeing something firsthand and that's what these people were determined to do.

It was the same centuries ago for shepherds out in the fields near Bethlehem. They had heard the awesome news that the Christ was born, the one whose coming their nation had looked forward to for so long, and they wanted to see him for themselves. It was not enough simply to hear the news from others, not even if they were angels; it called for a personal response, a firsthand experience.

The same is equally true for us today. If we would truly celebrate Christmas and fully respond to the good news of Christ, it is not enough merely to hear about him from others. Faith cannot be learned, any more than it can be inherited. The message of the gospel is that rather than just knowing about Jesus we can know him personally; instead of simply believing in God we can enter into a living relationship with him through his Spirit. It is a relationship that, like any, we need to continue cultivating each day, responding each moment from the heart. Have we done that? Do we still do it? Will we continue to do so over the Christmas season? The world-changing event of Christ's coming among us remains as real today as ever. Don't take my word for it – find out for yourself.

Pray

Living God,
   all too easily I turn faith into knowing *about* you
   rather than knowing you personally;
   into a matter of outward observance
   rather than inner response;
   into accepting what others say concerning you
   rather than rejoicing in a firsthand experience of your love.
I forget what should concern me most:
   that you want *my* response,
   my love,
   my commitment as much as any.
Forgive me for losing sight of that truth –
   for seeing the gospel in terms of others
   rather than me.
Forgive me for asking you to change to world
   but keeping myself out of the equation.
Save me from a second-hand discipleship –
   one that says more about what I'm meant to believe
   than what I believe in my heart.
Open my eyes to your presence,
   my ears to your word,
   my mind to your will,
   my heart to your grace
   and my spirit to your renewing touch.
Teach me to see and know that the gospel
   is not just good news for others
   but also good news for me,
   through Jesus Christ my Lord.
Amen.

Ponder

- How far is your faith a matter of personal experience, an ongoing relationship with God in Christ?
- Is it important to strike a balance between subjective experience and tradition? If so, why?
- What do you find most helpful in nurturing your relationship with Christ and keeping faith fresh?

Close

Lord Jesus Christ,
  come to me afresh each day
  and teach me to meet and greet you,
  so that I may know you as a friend and companion,
  serve you as my Saviour
  and confess you as the risen Lord,
  to the glory of your name.
Amen.

Day 6: A worshipful response

Approach

Lord Jesus Christ,
 I come,
 seeking to meet you,
 honour you
 and worship you.
Amen.

Read

Following the birth of Jesus in Bethlehem of Judea during the reign of King Herod, magi arrived in Jerusalem from the east, saying, 'Where is the one born king of the Jews, for we saw his star rising in the east and have come to pay our respects?' . . . As they entered the house they saw the child with his mother Mary, and, falling down in worship, they offered him their treasures: gifts of gold, frankincense and myrrh.
Matthew 2:1-2, 11

Reflect

If there's one thing we don't need, surely it's a reminder to make time for worship during the seasons of Advent and Christmas. Isn't this a time when more people worship than at any other time, churches up and down the country packed for festive services? Isn't it also a time when we ourselves will probably attend more services than usual: carol services, Christingle, Midnight Mass and so forth? Yet, paradoxically, meaningful worship can become sidelined at this time of year, in part because of these very services. It's the old story of familiarity bringing contempt. Not that we dismiss the importance of this season – on the contrary, for most people it is something special, possessing its own mystique. It's rather that everything about it has become so familiar – the readings, the carols, the format, the message – that we can end up going through the motions, singing carols almost for the sake of singing.

The response of the wise men to the birth of Jesus provides an important lesson for us all, for their response was above all one of worship. It's an astonishing picture: grown men – wise, wealthy, important – prostrating themselves in homage before a child, offering gifts in adoration. Yet for them this was the natural response, the only response they could make, for they instinctively realised that this child was special, unlike any other.

For us, of course, the truth of that is all the more apparent, for we recognise the Christ-child to be the Son of God, the one who came bringing light and life to all, the King of kings and Lord of lords, from whom all creation derives its being and in whom it will find its fulfilment. For such a person, only one response will do: a joyful outpouring of worship. As the well-loved carol puts it, 'Come and worship, worship Christ, the new-born King.' In all the celebrations of Christmas, all the frenetic activity, and, yes, even all the special services, don't forget to worship.

Pray

Well, that's it for another year, Lord.
It's all over, bar the shouting:
    the presents opened,
    the food eaten,
    the festivities winding down –
    back soon to the old routine.
It's been good,
    memorable in its way,
    yet I can't help feeling something's been missing –
    as though I've overlooked a vital detail,
    the most important job left undone.
That's it –
    I see it now:
    I've made time for feasting and fun,

for family and friends,
but I haven't made time for you,
to worship you as you deserve.
I've given you *some* time, of course,
more than usual, in fact,
sharing in all kinds of services to mark this festive season,
but they were as much about my edification as your glory,
about following tradition as much as following Christ.
I sang songs I've sung so often before
and barely considered their meaning.
I listened to words I've heard year after year
but scarcely taken them in.
I offered prayer,
but no longer expected to hear your voice.
Forgive me,
and remind me again of what Christmas is all about.
Break through the wrapping and trimmings,
the box into which we so neatly package you,
and help me again to see your love
in the child in a manger,
in the man on a cross,
in the risen, ascended Lord.
So may I offer my worship not as an afterthought
but as my first concern,
an instinctive spontaneous response,
offered to your praise and glory.
Amen.

Ponder

- Do carol and nativity services still carry for you a sense of worship? Is there a danger of tradition taking over so that events such as these become an end in themselves rather than a means of worshipping God?

- How far is your response in worship limited to church services? What part does personal devotion play in your day-to-day life?

Have you built such daily devotion into your Christmas cele-
brations?
* What ways have you explored to keep the message of Christmas, and your corresponding worship, fresh and meaningful?
Is there more you could and should be doing?

Close
Lord Jesus Christ,
    to you be praise and glory,
    honour and adulation,
    this day and always,
    for you are the Prince of Peace,
    the King of love,
    the giver of life,
    the Lord of all.
Receive my worship,
    and consecrate all I am to your service,
    for your name's sake.
Amen.

Day 7: A continuing response

Approach

Help me to see your face more clearly
  and to offer you not just these few moments now
  but the devotion of my heart always,
  through Jesus Christ my Lord.
Amen.

Read

In distant times and diverse ways, God spoke through the prophets to our forebears, but now, in these last times, he has spoken to us by a Son, through whom God created the universe and in whom we see a precise image of the divine nature, God's glory made manifest. Chosen to inherit all things and upholding all by his mighty word, he took his place at the right hand of the Sovereign on high, having offered cleansing for sins, and so, now, he is more exalted than angels, since he has inherited a title superior even to theirs. For did he say to any of the angels, 'You are my Son, born to me today'? Or, 'I will be a father to him and he a son to me'? . . . We need, then, to pay ever more attention to everything we have heard, to ensure that we do not wander from it.
Hebrews 1:1-6; 2:1

Reflect

'Will you still love me tomorrow?' So runs the haunting refrain of the 1960s hit song by The Shirelles. Originally posed in a love song, that question could equally be asked of us today by Jesus in relation to Christmas; a season when, more than any other, people are open to the gospel message; responsive, if only superficially, to the message of God's coming in Christ. Many will attend church for special services who would not otherwise dream of setting foot through the door. A good number will go further and receive the Eucharist at Christmas Eve Midnight Mass, thereby professing some kind of faith in Christ. Yet how many will be at church the following week? How many will spare Jesus a thought over the ensuing 52 weeks? And how many will attempt to relate the gospel in any meaningful way to their daily lives? Precious few.

Of course *we* will be among those few . . . or will we? We may profess the name of Christ and worship him week by week, but does the message of the gospel touch our lives in the way it once did? Is our faith as real and vibrant as the day when we first committed ourselves to his service? Do we still see discipleship in terms of a personal relationship, offering to Jesus our whole-hearted commitment and sacrificial service? Or does Christmas, together with the other key Christian festivals, represent a high point in our devotion, which for the most part is a matter of dutiful routine rather than joyful response?

True Christian discipleship is not about occasional bursts of fervour but about a lifetime of dedication, continuing in the faith whatever life might throw at us, running the race with persever-ance. That's why the writer to the Hebrews, having reminded his readers of the birth of Christ that set in motion the events of the gospel, went on to emphasise the importance of finishing what we've started. 'We need, then, to pay ever more attention to everything we have heard, to ensure that we do not wander from it' (Hebrews 2:1). I find myself thinking of another pop song, words sung by The Beatles: 'Will you still need me, will you still feed me, when I'm 64.' In other words, short-term commitment is one thing, long-term devotion quite another. Which of those two might best be used to describe our response to the good news of Jesus Christ?

Pray

Lord,
   it all seemed so easy at the time –
   a personal response,
   a public act of commitment,
   and it was done,
   my colours nailed to the mast,
   a Christian for all to see.
Only, of course, that wasn't the end to it but the beginning,
   the start of a twisting and sometimes testing road,
   calling for resilience,
   dedication,
   perseverance.
I've walked it, Lord,
   and want to keep on walking,
   but you know that at times I've faltered,
   stumbled,
   lost my way,
   even, on occasions, taken several steps back,
   and I worry that one day I might fall altogether –
   the way too hard,
   the challenge too steep,
   the lure of other paths too strong to resist.
Save me from that, I pray.
Walk with me, even if I go astray,
   pick me up should I fall,
   strengthen me should my spirits fail,
   and so may I press on until I reach my journey's end,
   the goal to which you have called me heavenwards,
   through Jesus Christ my Lord.
Amen.

Ponder

- How high will the birth of Jesus figure in your Christmas cele-brations this year? Will your response to Christ shape not only your Christmas festivities but also every aspect of life?
- Do you still see discipleship as a continuing journey?
- What obstacles have you encountered along the pathway of faith? What obstacles do you think you most need to be alert to in the future?

Close

Loving God,
    grant that the faith I profess in Christ
    might be as real tomorrow and every day as it is now.
Grant that, when Christmas is over,
    the good news at its heart will continue to shape my life
    and that I will carry on offering the one at its centre
    my wholehearted discipleship.
In his name I pray.
Amen.

Christmas week

A time to celebrate

The week ahead

Glad tidings, news of great joy for all people – such was the message proclaimed by the angels on the night of Jesus' birth. That of course is precisely what the word 'gospel' means – good news – but in what way was and is the birth of Christ good news for all? We put that question this week in terms of the experience of Mary, shepherds, wise men, Simeon and Anna, as well as the disadvantaged of this world, before returning finally to what the coming of Christ means to us today. The seasons of Advent and Christmas bring challenges that we cannot afford to ignore, but they give us, above all, cause for rejoicing, something to celebrate!

Day 1: Good news for the disadvantaged

Approach

Sovereign God,
   enlarge today the breadth of my vision
   and the parameters of my love,
   so that I might not only recognise
   that your love is good news for all
   but also understand what implications that has for my life
   and so respond accordingly,
   in the name of Christ.
Amen.

Read

He has toppled the rulers from their thrones and exalted the humble; he has filled the hungry with good things, and dismissed the affluent empty-handed.
Luke 1:52-53

Reflect

Do you remember the Band Aid single 'Feed the World', released in 1984 in response to unprecedented scenes of famine in Ethiopia? The words, written of course by Sir Bob Geldof, challenged the world not only to sit up and take notice but also to do something about the situation there, to respond with deeds as well as words. Between them, Band Aid and Live Aid stirred the hearts and minds of people across the world, offering a timely reminder that Christmas should be a joyful time for all, not just the few.

   As Christians, we should need no such reminder, for that truth is central to the message of the gospel. The song of Mary, for example, speaks of God exalting the humble and filling the hungry; words echoed by Jesus in his unforgettable words at the synagogue in Nazareth: 'God's Spirit is upon me,' he proclaims. 'He has anointed me to announce good news to the poor. He has sent me to declare liberty for the imprisoned and renewal of sight to the blind; to set free the subjugated; to broadcast the time of the Lord's blessing.' Passages such as these – reinforced by the example of Jesus throughout his ministry – have led many to make a stand for the disadvantaged of this world. South America, for instance, has seen the rise of so-called liberation theology, priests joining there with the poor in uprisings against oppression. In our own country, initiatives like Traidcraft have highlighted the importance of fair trade, causing multinational companies and corporations to review their practices. Within the Church, many have emphasised the importance of economic and social justice, Bishop David Sheppard going so far as to speak of God's *Bias to the Poor*. The gospel may not be reducible to social action, but a concern for the poor is integral to it, any faith that ignores their plight necessarily being defective.

The issues do not go away. Poverty remains an ugly scar on our world, in part caused by factors such as natural disaster and civil war, but most of all down to the harsh reality of exploitative market forces. We look forward to a time when things will be different; a time when justice will prevail, the poor will no longer be taken advantage of, and human deprivation will be a thing of the past, but we cannot leave it there. We have a responsibility in this life to respond, not just in prayer but also in deeds, doing whatever we can, no matter how small, to work for a fairer world in which the dignity and rights of all will be respected. For all who profess the name of Christ there should be no need to ask twice, least of all in this season of goodwill: what are we doing to bring good news to the poor and disadvantaged of this world?

Pray

I sang carols, Lord, and offered my worship.
I sent cards and handed out presents.
I ate, drank and made merry,
    celebrating,
    giving thanks,
    rejoicing in another Christmas season.
Only then I saw the scenes on the news,
    the report in the paper,
    the faces on the poster –
    images of drought and famine, hunger and disease:
    bellies swollen,
    limbs protruding,
    eyes glazed over in dull despair,
    bodies limp and lifeless –
    and I knew that *you* were not rejoicing,
    but crying out for help,
    calling me to respond from my plenty to their need,
    to give to you through giving to them,
    to celebrate Christmas by helping others to celebrate life.
How could I forget, Lord?
How could I respond to the greatest gift ever given
    with self-indulgence,
    extravagance,
    greed;
    my worship saying one thing,
    my life another;
    good news for all turned to good news for me.
Forgive me,
    and teach me to make room for both:
    to sing carols and offer worship,
    to send cards and give presents,
    to eat, drink and be merry,
    but also to reach out to a world in need
    and to respond in love,
        in Jesus' name.
Amen.

Ponder

- If God is love, why does he allow poverty, injustice and exploitation? How would you answer this kind of argument? In what ways does the answer you give have implications for your own response to the disadvantaged of this world?
- What situations of human need are you currently aware of? In what practical ways might you respond?
- How often do you make a point of praying for the disadvantaged? Do you sometimes use prayer as an excuse to avoid a more concrete and costly response to their needs?

Close

Loving Lord,
   teach me not just to speak of your love for all
   but to act upon it,
   responding and giving sacrificially to those in need
   as an expression of gratitude
   for everything you so freely sacrificed for me.
Amen.

Day 2: Good news for those who seek

Approach

Almighty God,
  I look for your guidance,
  I seek your will,
  I search for wisdom and understanding.
Direct me by your Spirit,
  so that I may discover more of your purpose
  and discern your gracious love
  within the complexities and riddles of this life,
  and in the joy of life to come.
Amen.

Read

Following the birth of Jesus in Bethlehem of Judea during the reign of King Herod, magi arrived in Jerusalem from the east, saying, 'Where is the one born king of the Jews, for we saw his star rising in the east and have come to pay our respects?'
Matthew 2:1-2

Reflect

'Seek, and you will find,' said Jesus, and for the wise men that turned out to be true. When they saw the rising of a star in the East and took this to indicate the birth of a king, they set off to find him, eager to pay homage and to ascertain what sort of king he might be. Details of their journey are sketchy, to say the least. We have no way of knowing if it was long or short, direct or circuitous, straightforward or demanding. All we know is that, arriving initially in Jerusalem – presumably assuming that, as the capital city, this was the obvious place to look – they were directed to Bethlehem, where, to their delight, they found the object of their search: the child Jesus. They had searched and they had found.

Do *we* always find, in turn? That, of course, depends very much on what we are looking for. How about, then, in terms solely of faith: is our searching there always successful? For many the answer would have to be no, or at least not in this life. Many Christians wrestle with questions that they cannot resolve, issues that, though not necessarily precluding faith, at times threaten to undermine it. Others never feel able to reach a point of commitment, much though they would like to. They want to believe, but they can't – or, at least, they can't fully accept everything that the Church declares is essential to true discipleship. So they carry on searching for answers, some continuing to do so until their dying day. Are those who question in this way disqualified from God's kingdom? Does their inability to unreservedly dedicate their lives to Christ put them beyond the scope of his grace? Surely not! If they are honest with themselves and with him, I cannot imagine that God will do anything other than honour that, drawing them gladly to himself and leading them finally to the answers they have pursued for so long. 'Seek, and you will find,' said Jesus, and in that, I believe, is not just a promise but also a tacit endorsement of the need to keep looking for answers until we find them. The end of that search may not perhaps come swiftly, not even some-times in this life, but it *will* come – we have his word.

Pray

Lord,
  there is so much I don't understand,
  so much that, if I'm honest, troubles me:
  questions concerning evil and suffering,
  the nature of truth and authority of Scripture;
  uncertainties concerning the origins of life
  and our ultimate goal;
  doubts over matters of creed and doctrine,
  even sometimes your very existence.
I'm don't question lightly, far from it,

for such things strike at the heart of my faith,
threatening everything I believe –
or, at least, everything I'm meant to believe –
yet I can't help it,
for there's no use pretending,
no point claiming everything is all right when it clearly isn't.
I might fool others,
    but not you,
    or me,
    so where would that get us?
No,
    I can only continue searching,
    looking for answers for as long as it takes,
    trusting that one day, in your own time,
    the quest will be over,
    the journey complete,
    the understanding I seek finally granted.
Until then, Lord,
    go with me,
    lead me,
    teach me.
Show me, as you have promised, that those who seek *will* find!
Amen.

Ponder

- Are there aspects of faith you still struggle with? Do you worry sometimes that the doubts and questions you have mean that you're not in fact a Christian, or at least not as much a Christian as you should be?

- Do you know anyone personally who is searching for faith yet feels unable to overcome the obstacles preventing him/her from making a commitment? What sort of advice would you give to that person? How would you cope in his/her place?

- To whom or what do you turn for understanding concerning

the things of God? Are you still willing to search for deeper insight into aspects of faith that puzzle you, or do you attempt to blot these out?

Close

Gracious God,
for the assurance that in you I will find the meaning I seek,
the end of all my striving,
receive my praise.
May that truth inspire
and instruct my continuing search for understanding
until that day I see and know you face to face,
and all is answered,
through Jesus Christ my Lord.
Amen.

Day 3: Good news for those who wait

Approach

Faithful God,
   unfold to me your guidance,
   your word,
   your will,
   so that I may walk in faith,
   leaving all in your hands,
   confident that your will shall be done,
   and your kingdom come,
   through Jesus Christ my Lord.
Amen.

Read

There was a man called Simeon in Jerusalem who was upright and devout, eagerly awaiting the consolation of Israel, and the Holy Spirit was with him. The Spirit had disclosed to him that he would not taste death before he had seen the Lord's Messiah. Led by the Spirit, Simeon entered the temple; and when Jesus' parents brought in their child to honour the customs of the Law, Simeon cradled him in his arms and praised God, saying, 'Master, now let your servant go in peace, according to your promise. With my own eyes I have seen the salvation you have prepared before all the world – a light that will reveal you to the Gentiles and bring glory to your people Israel.'
Luke 2:25-32

Reflect

'All things come to those who wait' – so says the old proverb, but is that true? Taken literally, the answer has to be no: many wait in vain for aspirations to be realised, their hopes and expectations all too often dashed. But, of course, this is to misunderstand the thrust of the saying. Its point is that sometimes we need to be patient if our dreams are to be fulfilled, ready to do our bit and then to wait for as long as it takes for our efforts to bear fruit.

There is something of this idea in the story of Simeon, only the promise here concerns not any efforts we might make but what God has done and promised to do. Simeon, we are told, had been assured he would not taste death until he saw the day of the Messiah. Why he was granted this honour we are not told, but perhaps the patience Simeon showed in waiting gives us a clue. Many, in his position, would have lost heart as the years went by, their confidence dwindling, their sense of expectation growing less by the day, but not so with Simeon. He waited faithfully, trusting despite his ever-advancing years that what God had promised would indeed happen, and so finally it was to prove.

We need to be careful how we apply this today. It does not mean that if we ask God for something and then wait patiently enough it is guaranteed to happen. As I have said, many of us will know from painful experience that this is not so. We can beg God to do something, implore him day after day, and yet wait in vain, the only answer God seeming to give being a resounding 'No!' Sometimes that may indeed be his answer, but it may equally be that the answer is 'Not yet, have patience, wait until the time is right.' We cannot be sure, for we rarely if ever know beyond all doubt whether something is God's will or simply autosuggestion: us imposing our own wishes upon him. What the experience of Simeon counsels us, however, is that God's purpose will finally triumph come what may, nothing finally able to frustrate his will. We need to trust his timing, recognising that it may not correspond to our own, holding firm to the conviction that, by his grace, good things come to those who wait.

Pray

What's happening, Lord?
When are you going to hear me?
You can't say I haven't been patient,
for it's not just been months now but years –
long frustrating years of waiting,
longing,
hoping –
and still no sign of an answer.
I've kept faith –
or at least I've tried to –
but it's not easy,
not easy at all,
for didn't you say, 'Ask, and you will receive',
'Seek, and you will find'?
Well, I've asked,
I've sought,
and I'm still seeking,
but there's no sign of much happening,
no suggestion you're about to respond.
Lord,
help me to be patient,
to recognise that your timing is not the same as mine.
Help me to trust,
putting faith in your purpose rather than mine.
Teach me that you *do* hear
and you *will* answer,
but when and where is down to you,
and in that assurance may I find the strength to wait
for as long as you ask.
Amen.

Ponder

- Do you show sufficient patience in prayer, or do you expect God to grant what you ask almost as soon as you ask him?
- Do you give up in prayer too easily?
- How can you decide whether God is saying no to a request or simply calling you to wait longer before he grants it?

Close

Eternal God,
    ruler of history,
    Lord of space and time,
    teach me to wait upon you, now and always,
    trusting that, though I may not always see it,
    you are constantly at work,
    bringing your saving purpose to fulfilment in Christ.
In his name, I ask it.
Amen.

Day 4: Good news for the sorrowful

Approach

Living God,
   I come as I am,
   bringing life as it is,
   assured that your love extends to the whole person,
   touching everything we might experience:
   the good and the bad,
   the happy and the sad.
Speak your word,
   and show me that, whatever each day might bring,
   you will be at work within it,
   ministering your love in Christ.
Amen.

Read

Similarly, there was a prophetess called Anna, a daughter of Phanuel of the tribe of Asher. She was of a great age, having lived with her husband seven years after the day of her marriage, and then as a widow until the age of eighty-four, during the latter time not once having left the temple but having served God there through prayer and fasting night and day. Entering at that very moment, she gave thanks to God and spoke of the child to all those in Jerusalem who were waiting for redemption.
Luke 2:36-38

Reflect

The story of Anna is usually seen as a virtual parallel to that of Simeon, both held up as paradigms of patience as they waited faithfully for the fulfilment of God's promises. There is, though, another aspect to Anna that we might overlook; namely, that for

143

most of her life she lived as a widow, having endured the trauma of bereavement after just seven years of marriage. In other words, she was one who had tasted the pain of sorrow, not just sadness but a grief that pierces the very soul. Her response had been to dedicate herself to God, serving him day and night from that point onwards in a life of prayer and fasting. Did that strict regime bring her happiness? Who can say? She may well have found solace in the rhythms and worship of temple life; equally, she may have imposed this rigorous discipline on herself as a way of blotting out the deeper pain she felt within. Whatever the case, tears were not finally to have the last word, for as she went about her daily routine, suddenly she recognised in the child Jesus the answer not just to her own needs but also to those of her people, the fulfilment of God's loving redemptive purpose for all the world. How she knew Jesus to be the Messiah we do not know, but suddenly her life was filled with joy, her heart overflowing with thanksgiving, life taking on new meaning.

Her story presents in microcosm a truth that we see illustrated repeatedly in the Gospels, whether that was through restoring of sight to the blind, health to the sick, loved ones to the bereaved or hope to the despairing. Unerringly, Jesus reached out in compassion, ministering his love and turning sorrow into joy. This is not to minimise the pain of tragedy or to pretend that the scars are quickly healed. Anyone who has suffered the loss of a loved one or any personal calamity will know that the grieving process can be long and painful and that in this life the wounds sometimes never fully heal. To one in the throes of such a time it can seem as though light will never shine again, hope never be reborn, yet God has promised that those who mourn shall be comforted, those who weep shall laugh. He promises that his love will always be there to support us, even through the valley of the shadow of death. There are no easy answers to grief, no quick fixes to sorrow, but at the heart of our faith is the conviction that God shares it with us and will ultimately lead us through.

Pray

'Rejoice in the Lord always' –
    isn't that what we're told to do?
'Give thanks in all circumstances.'
'Make music in your hearts.'
Well, that's what I've done, Lord –
    most of the time, anyway –
    life being good to me,
    with so much to celebrate,
    so many reasons to give you thanks.
But now it's different,
    for I've come face to face with sorrow,
    grief no longer about others but about me.
I've felt the agony of loss,
    the pain of separation,
    and where flowers once bloomed life has become a desert.
I've tasted the gall of loneliness,
    the bitterness of tears,
    and where wine once flowed now there is only vinegar.
It's been hard to praise you through that, Lord,
    to sing a new song,
    to make a joyful noise,
    for I've been heavy within,
    the sparkle gone not just from life but also from faith.
Yet even there, in the darkness, I have glimpsed your face,
    your hand leading me through,
    and I realise now, as light beckons once more,
    that you were there with me all along,
    as you are with me always,
    bearing my sorrow,
    sharing my pain,
    not expecting me to laugh through the tears
    but gently wiping them away,
    easing the hurt and bandaging up my wounds.
Lord, for your faithfulness even in the darkest moments,
    your love that will not let me go,

receive my glad thanksgiving,
in the name of Christ.
Amen.

Ponder

- Is it possible to have joy without sorrow? What are the implications of your answer in terms of life as we know it?
- Has tragedy every threatened to undermine your faith? How do you make sense of sorrow in terms of Christian belief?
- In what ways have you found strength and support in times of sorrow? How important has your faith been to you in seeing you through?

Close

Gracious God,
reach out to our broken and bleeding world,
and bind up its wounds.
Reach out to those who are sorrowful and hurting,
and bring comfort deep within.
Reach out to all who walk through the valley of tears
and bring the assurance
that those who mourn will one day laugh –
that, by your grace, tears will give way to laughter,
and despair to delight.
Amen.

Day 5: Good news to ponder

Approach

Living God,
  I come to reflect,
  to make a space in my life for you to speak to me.
Help me to hear your voice,
  to listen,
  and to respond.
Amen.

Read

Mary stored these things up in her heart, pondering what they might mean. [She] treasured deep within everything that had happened.
Luke 2:19, 51b

Reflect

Ask people what Christmas means to them and you are likely to get a variety of answers. For some it is an opportunity for family get-togethers; for others an excuse to eat, drink and make merry; for others again the chance to watch hours of television; for others still a sentence to slavery in the kitchen preparing and clearing up after a seemingly never-ending sequence of meals and festive fare; and for others still an occasion for carol singing, nativity plays and candlelight services. What all these have in common is that they involve some kind of activity, whether of the couch-potato variety – sitting and watching – or of a more arduous nature – cooking, cleaning, washing-up. The one thing all too few will probably find time for is an opportunity to pause and ponder, a few moments in which to step aside from the hustle and bustle and reflect on what this season, and indeed life itself, is all about.

In our ever more hectic world, with its frequently frenetic pace of life, that's hard to do at the best of times, but especially so at Christmas. There's simply so much to do: presents to buy, cards to write, food to prepare, decorations to put up, parties to organise, programmes to watch, stockings to fill, and so much else, never mind the Advent and Christmas services that many of us will want to share in. And then, of course, before we know it, there are the New Year sales, to which people flock in their droves, eager to snap up a bargain, to spend the money they've received as presents, or simply to indulge their desire to spend. Small wonder that many find Christmas exhausting to the point of being glad when it's all over.

What a contrast there is between this picture and that we are given of Mary following the birth of Jesus. Twice we are told of her reactions, and each time her response is essentially the same. What was it? Did she fret and worry over Jesus, afraid he might catch a chill out there in the stable? Did she get in a tizzy when the shepherds arrived, trying to make herself look presentable? Did she bombard Joseph with instructions concerning what he should and shouldn't do? Not as far as we know, she didn't. Instead, she pondered all that had happened, quietly reflecting on the momentous events she was privileged to be part of, treasuring them in her heart. She made time, in other words, to think, to consider, to ask what it all meant; and to mull over what significance it might have in terms of daily life. Do we do that at Christmas? Do we consciously set aside quality time in which to focus on the reason behind our festivities? Do we step back from the commotion to consider what God might be saying to us? Do we make room for Jesus somewhere in our celebrations? It's not easy, I know, for there is so much else we need to do and so much that is expected of us, but it's well worth making the effort, for only then will Christmas really speak to us in the way we hope; only then will it have the power to satisfy us in body, mind and spirit.

Pray

What does it mean, Lord:
  all this hustle and bustle,
  buying and spending?
Why have I spent these last few weeks chasing my tail,
  rushing here, there and everywhere,
  sending cards,
  wrapping presents,
  buying food,
  singing carols?
I enjoy these – don't get me wrong –
  each in their way
  a part of the Christmas I've grown to know and love,
  but occasionally it all seems just that bit too frenetic:
  so much to be done
  yet not so much idea why we do it.
I *do* know, Lord, of course I do,
  only I can't help being distracted:
  the truth at the heart of this season –
  the gift of your love –
  crowded out by other matters,
  each seeming so pressing at the time
  yet ultimately of such little concern.
Forgive me, Lord, for thinking of everything and everyone . . .
  except you,
  for focusing on so much trivia . . .
  and losing sight of what really counts.
Teach me to celebrate all that is good in this season,
  but also to distinguish the froth from the substance,
  the wrapping from the gift,
  the glitter from the gold.
Teach me to step back,
  to pause,
  and to ponder,
  and so may I find meaning not just in today
  but every day,

not just at Christmas
but always.
Amen.

Ponder

• How often do you make time for quiet reflection, simply to sit quietly in the presence of God? Will you make a point of ensuring you have such quality time this Christmas?

• Does the Christmas message still speak to you as it used to, or has it become so familiar that it tends to wash over you?

• When did you last carefully read the biblical accounts of the nativity and then ponder what they might have to say to you today?

Close

Living God,
    teach me not only today but equally every day
    to make time for you,
    and to find space in my life
    to reflect on everything you do, have done and shall do.
So may I understand more fully the magnitude of your love
    and the awesomeness of everything you offer us in Christ,
    in whose name I pray.
Amen.

Day 6: Good news to share

Approach

Living God,
    speak to me now,
    so that I may speak for you.
Come to me now,
    so that I may go out in your name,
    and live for you always.
Amen.

Read

They came with haste, and found Mary and Joseph, and the baby lying in a manger. Having seen it, they shared everything they had been told concerning the child, and all those who heard them marvelled at what the shepherds said.
Luke 2:16-18

Reflect

One of the gifts I treasure, working from home, is being able to meet my children after school. Each day my daughter runs out with something new to show me, just as my son used to do a few years earlier. Sometimes it is a new book she has read that day, sometimes a picture she has drawn, sometimes a piece of craftwork, or some-times simply a letter from the teacher. Whatever it is, she is always bursting to show it, eyes alight with excitement. Similarly, the walk home is illumined by news of the day's events: games played, friends made, work done. There is always something to share.

We see something of that same spontaneity and exuberance in the example of the shepherds in Luke 2. We left them last having hurried to the stable to see if everything the angel had said was true – whether the Messiah had indeed been born. Now, having confirmed that, they hurry away with equal purpose and enthusi-asm, impulsively glorifying and praising God as they share what they had been told concerning the child. Their experience that night was not something to keep to themselves but to be shouted from the rooftops, and I've no doubt that friends, family and anyone else they came across were treated to a full account of everything they had heard and seen.

They were not the only ones to find that meeting Jesus led them to tell others about it in turn. A leper he had healed (Mark 1) was instructed to tell no one about it, but he simply could not help himself. 'He hurried away,' we read, 'and proceeded to declare openly what had happened, spreading the news far and wide, so that, before long, Jesus dared not enter any town for fear of being recognised, keeping instead to the countryside; but even here crowds flocked to him from all sides' (Mark 1:45). Philip responded to the call to follow Jesus, and straightaway rushed off to find his friend Nathanael, eager to tell him what had happened. A woman from Samaria, having met with Jesus at a well, hurries back to her home city, and the next thing we know 'Many Samaritans from that city came to faith in him because of what the woman had told them' (John 4:39a). Peter and John were hauled before the Jewish authorities and reprimanded for preaching about Jesus, formally warned that it would be the worse for them if they persisted in doing so, but they defiantly reply, 'We cannot keep from speaking of the things that we have seen and heard' (Acts 4:20).

We, of course, have not seen and heard in quite the same way as these did, for we were not privileged to meet Jesus in the flesh or to witness his earthly ministry, but we have experienced his love, nonetheless, our lives touched by his Spirit and each day transformed by his grace. Faith is not simply about what he has done for others but also about what he has done and continues to do for us. Do we see that as good news to share? Do our eyes sparkle with a child's enthusiasm to pass it on? Do we yearn to make known what *we* have seen and heard? God has given us good news in Christ: what are we doing with it?

Pray

Lord Jesus Christ,
  you call me to witness to others,
  to make known what you have done for me,
  and I want to do just that:
  to tell of your gracious love
  and to share how much you mean to me,
  only I'm not sure where,
  or when,
  or how.
I don't want to preach at others,
  to force my beliefs down their throats.
I don't want to push religion,
  spouting on about faith at every moment.
I want to talk naturally,
  impulsively,
  speaking of you when it is right to do so,
  testifying at the appropriate time and place,
  in a meaningful way,
  so that *my* words ring true
  and *your* word hits home.
But it's not easy, Lord,
  for we're up today against so many preconceptions
  and stereotypes,
  such that what we say is rarely what is heard.
Teach me, then, what *you* would have me say
  and help me to say it,
  sensitively, spontaneously and sincerely,
  to the glory of your name.
Amen.

Ponder

- How would you sum up what God has done for you? What, for you, is following Jesus all about? In what way would you say knowing and serving him makes a difference to your life?
- What do you find hardest about sharing the gospel? Do you think there are any factors specific to our modern age that make witnessing to Christ more difficult than it might once have been? How might we get over such problems?
- How do you think you can most effectively share your faith? What aspects of the gospel would you most want to emphasise?

Close

Lord Jesus Christ,
　　you have made yourself known to me:
　　help me to make you known to others,
　　so that they may share in the joy and experience the love
　　you so long to impart to all.
Amen.

Day 7: Good news to celebrate

Approach

Gracious God,
for the joy of loving you and of being loved,
receive my praise.
Amen.

Read

There were shepherds in that area, living in the fields and keeping watch over their flock during the night. Suddenly, an angel of the Lord appeared to them, and the glory of the Lord shone around them, and they were petrified. However, the angel said to them, 'No need to be afraid; see, I am bringing you wonderful news of immeasurable joy for all people: today a Saviour has been born to you in the city of David, who is Christ the Lord. Let this be a sign to you: you will find a child swaddled in strips of cloth and lying in a manger.' All at once, there was with the angel rank on rank of other heavenly beings, praising God and saying, 'Glory to God in the highest heaven, and peace on earth among all on whom his favour rests!'
Luke 2:8-14

Reflect

We have looked at many aspects of Advent and Christmas over the last few weeks, recognising that these combined seasons touch almost every aspect of life. They speak of promise but also of challenge, of mercy but also of judgement, of gift but also of response. They bring home the love God has for us but also the love he has for others that we are called to show in turn, witnessing to our faith through word and deed. All this, and much more, is what Advent and Christmas would say to us, but if there is one aspect I would choose as paramount, one truth that I would urge you to take away, it is that God want us to celebrate. That, surely, is the heart of the gospel, repeatedly emerging from the texts associated with these seasons. 'You have multiplied the nation,' writes Isaiah (9:3), 'you have increased its joy; they rejoice before you as with joy at the harvest, as people exult when dividing plunder.' 'My soul magnifies the Lord,' sings Mary (Luke 1:46-47), 'and my spirit exults in God my Saviour.' 'No need to be afraid,' says the angel (Luke 2:10), 'see, I am bringing you wonderful news of immeasurable joy for all people.' And so we could go on. Shepherds go on their way, praising God. Wise men offer their gifts in worship, overjoyed to find the Christ-child. Simeon and Anna exult when Jesus is brought to the temple, their hopes and prayers concerning the coming of the Messiah answered. Likewise, countless millions across the years have rejoiced in turn, celebrating what God has done for them, revelling in the new life he offers in Christ. They, like us, lived far from perfect lives. Their service has sometimes been flawed, their faith weak, their love partial and their commitment compromised, but they offered their discipleship nonetheless, knowing that God values it because he values them. He does not expect us to be faultless either; he asks simply that we come to him and respond as best we can to his love. That, surely, is good news to celebrate!

Pray

Gracious God,
  I lose sight sometimes of what discipleship is all about,
  of your gift at the heart of the gospel –
  a joy beyond words,
  bubbling up within me,
  brimful,
  overflowing.
I brood instead on faults and failings,
  worry about the weakness of my love,
  wrestle with matters of doctrine,

and fret over the cost of discipleship,
forgetting that though these are all part of commitment
they are not the whole,
and not finally what matters most.
Remind me that you accept me as I am,
    your love not earned but given.
Remind me that though I repeatedly let you down,
    still you stay faithful,
    nothing able to exhaust your grace.
Remind me that though the old self lives on,
    you are constantly making all things new,
    offering life in abundance,
    now and for all eternity.
Gracious God,
    I pause,
    I reflect,
    I remember the wonder of your love,
    and so once more I celebrate with heart and mind and soul.
This day, like all days, is your gift:
    I will rejoice and be glad in it.
Amen.

Ponder

- Does your life reflect the joy you claim to have found in Christ?
- Are there aspects of discipleship you tend sometimes to focus on at the cost of celebrating new life in Christ? What are they? Why is it that you lose your sense of proportion over such things?
- In what way does the joy we speak of as Christians differ from what we might term 'everyday happiness'? How, for example, can such joy survive after our lives have been touched by tragedy and corresponding heartbreak?

Close

God of joy,
   put a song in my mouth,
   a smile on my lips,
   laughter in my eyes
   and celebration in my heart,
   this and every day.
Amen.